STRIPES

VEERA VÄLIMÄKI

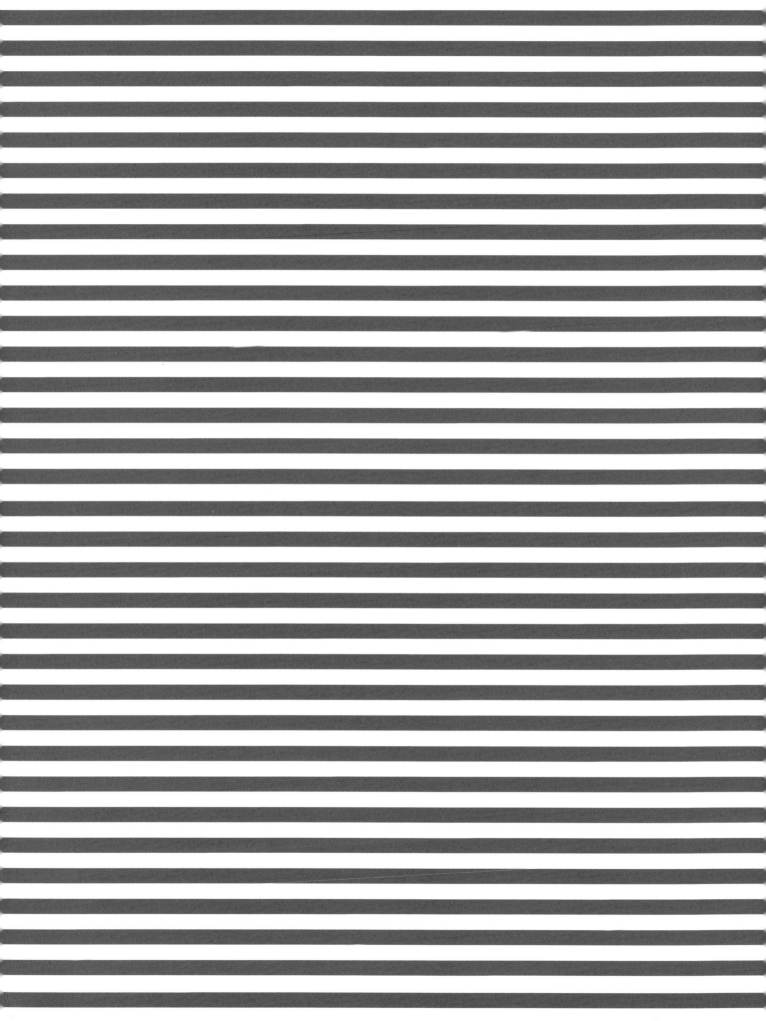

LAINE

STRIPES

VEERA VÄLIMÄKI

Hardie Grant

BOOKS

FOREWORD

I have always loved stripes. I adore stripes in clothes, on different surfaces, in nature, but most of all, I love knitting them. I have talked about stripes with so many people, told stories about stripes in my past as well as taught numerous classes. Now I'm happy to find stripes on the pages of this book.

The inspiration for this book comes from many things close to me: clear lakes, the shimmering sea, deep green forests and stony ground covered in moss. I cannot claim to be a true outdoors person, but nature has had a great impact in creating this book. I see stripes in the waves of the nearby lake, I see them in snowdrifts around the house. I see stripes in the distant landscape, where the trees align layer after layer, I see them in the mist moving across the fields. I can also see stripes in the planking of a house and in the way windows are set on a façade. Different surroundings have always been important to me.

This book has been a true adventure. While working on these pages, my world has changed more than I ever could have guessed. I don't think I am alone in feeling like this, as the year 2020 was a step towards the unknown for everyone. The first notes about this book are even further away, I found them in a notebook from 2018. For a long time, this book only existed in my dreams and in those few scribbles on those half-hidden pages. I didn't want to rush the process. Finally, the right time came, under the warm sun of the French countryside, and suddenly the book started to feel like something I could turn into reality. I am forever grateful for the time given to this book.

This book is filled with views and places and memories. You can see the clear water of lake Puujärvi, the narrow paths in the forests, the sheep in the meadows nearby and the flat, never-ending views of my childhood in western Finland. The names of the designs also reflect the past. I wanted to name them after famous Finnish female artists and my grandmothers.

Stripes always seem to cheer me up. Even after more than a decade of knitting them, I am excited to knit some more. I am forever fascinated by the endless possibilities in choosing the colours and imagining the projects coming to life. I simply adore the hours and hours spent with my happily clicking needles, while dreaming about the finished knit. I hope these small things can bring you joy, too.

I hope this book helps you to start your own journey into the world of stripes. I hope you will find ideas, dreams and maybe even your new favourite knit on these pages. Thank you for joining me on this journey of Stripes.

Veera

ABBREVIATIONS

approx.	Approximately
bef	Before
beg	Begin(ning)
BO	Bind off
BOR	Beginning of the round
CC	Contrast(ing) colour
CN	Cable needle
CO	Cast on
cont	Continue(s), continuing
dec('d)	Decrease/decreasing (/decreased)
DPN(S)	Double-pointed needle(s)
DS	Double stitch: Slip the next stitch with yarn in front. Bring the yarn over the right needle to the back and pull on the slipped stitch until it looks like double stitch (two legs).
est	Establish(ed)
foll	Following
inc('d)	Increase(d)
k	Knit
k2tog	Knit 2 stitches together [1 stitch decreased]
k2tog tbl	Knit 2 stitches together through back loops [1 stitch decreased]
kds	Knit double stitch: Knit both legs together.
k1fb	Knit into the front and back of a stitch [1 stitch increased]
k1fbf	Knit into the front, back and again into the front of a stitch [2 stitches increased]
k1tbl	Knit through back loop of the stitch (twisted stitch)
kwise	Knitwise
LH	Left hand
m	Marker
m1l(p)	Make 1 left: With your left-hand needle pick up the bar between the last stitch you knitted (purled) and the next stitch on the left-hand needle, bringing the needle from the front to the back, knit (purl) into the back of the stitch you just picked up. [1 stitch increased]
m1r(p)	Make 1 right: With your left-hand needle pick up the bar between the last stitch you knitted (purled) and the next stitch on the left-hand needle, bringing the needle from the back to the front, knit (purl) into the front of the stitch you just picked up. [1 stitch increased]
MC	Main colour
p	Purl
p2tog	Purl 2 stitches together [1 stitch decreased]
p2tog tbl	Purl 2 stitches together through back loops [1 stitch decreased]

patt	Pattern
pl	Place
PM	Place marker
p1tbl	Purl through back loop (twisted stitch)
PUW	Pick up wrap: Insert right needle upwards through the wrap around the bottom of the next stitch and the front leg of the next stitch. On a purl row, insert right needle from the back of your work through the wrap around the bottom of the next stitch and the front leg of the next stitch. Purl the two loops as if they were one stitch. On a knit row, insert needle from the front of your work. Knit the two loops as if they were one stitch.
pwise	Purlwise
rem	Remain(ing)
rep	Repeat
RH	Right hand
RM	Remove marker
rnd(s)	Round(s)
RS	Right side of fabric
sl	Slip (purlwise with yarn in back on RS and yarn in front on WS, unless otherwise stated)
SM	Slip marker
ssk	Slip, slip, knit: Slip 2 stitches one at a time as if to knit, knit them together through back loops. [1 stitch decreased]

ssp	Slip, slip, purl: Slip 2 stitches one at a time as if to knit, purl them together through back loops. [1 stitch decreased]
sssk	Slip, slip, slip, knit: Slip 3 stitches one at a time as if to knit, knit them together through back loops. [2 stitches decreased]
st(s)	Stitch(es)
St st	Stockinette stitch
tbl	Through the back loop
tog	Together
tw	Turn work
WS	Wrong side of fabric
wyib	With yarn in back
wyif	With yarn in front
w&t	Wrap & turn: Slip the next stitch on your left needle to the right needle. If you are on a knit row, bring the yarn from back to front; if you are on a purl row, bring the yarn from front to back. Slip the stitch back to your left needle so that the yarn "wraps" that stitch, then turn your work so the other side is facing you.
yds	Yards
yo	Yarn over: Bring yarn between needles to the front, then over right-hand needle ready to knit the next stitch [1 stitch increased]
–	Repeat from * to *
()	Repeat from (to)

Kyllikki

We all need those trusty companions, sometimes even in the form of fabric! This cardigan sure is a wardrobe staple, which you will love and wear year after year.

KYLLIKKI is the cardigan of my dreams; it is simple yet elegant, light yet warm.

SIZES

1 (2, 3, 4, 5, 6, 7, 8, 9)

Shown in size 3. Recommended ease: 8" / 20 cm of positive ease.

FINISHED MEASUREMENTS

Bust Circumference: 40 (44, 48, 52, 56, 60, 64, 68, 72)" / 100 (110, 120, 130, 140, 150, 160, 170, 180) cm.
Upper Arm Circumference: 11 (11.5, 12.5, 13, 14.5, 16, 17.5, 19, 21)" / 27 (29, 31, 33, 36, 40, 44, 48, 52) cm.
Armhole Depth: 9.5 (10.5, 11, 12, 13, 14, 15, 15.5, 16)" / 24 (26, 28, 30, 32, 35, 37, 39, 40) cm.
Body Length (from underarm) (all sizes): 16" / 40 cm.
Sleeve Length (from underarm) (all sizes): 16" / 40 cm.
Cuff Circumference: 7 (7.5, 8, 9, 10, 11, 12, 13, 14.5)" / 18 (19, 20, 24, 25, 28, 32, 34, 36) cm.

MATERIALS

Yarn: 4 (4, 4, 5, 5, 6, 6, 7, 7) skeins of Tukuwool Fingering by Tukuwool (100% Finnish wool, 220 yds / 200 m – 50 g), colourway Runo as main colour (MC).

Or approx. 720 (790, 870, 980, 1080, 1180, 1280, 1400, 1650) yds / 660 (720, 790, 900, 990, 1080, 1170, 1280, 1380, 1510) m of fingering weight yarn.

3 (3, 3, 4, 4, 4, 5, 5, 5) skeins of Tukuwool Fingering by Tukuwool (100% Finnish wool, 220 yds / 200 m – 50 g), colourway Rae as contrasting colour (CC). Or approx. 500 (550, 610, 690, 850, 940, 1050) yds / 460 (500, 560, 630, 700, 770, 860, 960) m of fingering weight yarn.

Needles: US 2 / 2.75 mm 32" / 80 cm circular needles and US 4 / 3.5 mm 32" / 80 cm circular needles and DPNs for sleeves in each size if not using magic loop method for short circumference knitting, or size needed to obtain the gauge.

Notions: 4 buttons, 1" / 25 mm. Stitch markers, stitch holders or waste yarn, tapestry needle, row counter.

GAUGE

22 sts x 30 rows to 4" / 10 cm on US 4 / 3.5 mm needles in Stockinette stitch, after blocking.

DIRECTIONS

SHOULDER INCREASES

Using US 4 / 3.5 mm needles and MC, CO 44 (44, 44, 46, 46, 48, 48, 50, 50) sts. Do not join. Purl the first row.

Row 1 (RS): K1, m1r, PM, p1, m1l, knit to last 2 sts, m1r, p1, PM, m1l, k1.
Row 2 (WS): Purl to marker, m1lp, SM, k1, m1rp, purl to 1 st before marker, m1lp, k1, SM, m1rp, purl to end.
Row 3 (RS): Knit to marker, m1r, SM, p1, m1l, knit to 1 st before marker, m1r, p1, SM, m1l, knit to end.
Row 4 (WS): Purl to marker, m1lp, SM, k1, m1rp, purl to 1 st before marker, m1lp, k1, SM, m1rp, purl to end.
Row 5 (RS): K3, m1l, knit to marker, m1r, SM, p1, m1l, knit to 1 st before marker, m1r, p1, SM, m1l, k to last 3 sts, m1r, k3.
Row 6 (WS): Purl to marker, m1lp, SM, k1, m1rp, purl to 1 st before marker, m1lp, k1, SM, m1rp, purl to end.

Repeat rows 3–6, (8, 10, 11, 12, 13, 15, 16, 17) more times.

Sizes 1 (–, –, 4, –, –, –, 8, –): Work row 3 once. Purl to end on next row (WS), knitting the single reverse St st stitches next to markers.
Sizes – (2, –, –, 5, –, –, –, 9): Work rows 3–4 once.
Sizes – (–, –, –, –, 6, –, –, –): Work rows 3–5 once. Purl to end on next row (WS) knitting the single reverse St st stitches next to markers..

After all shoulder increases you should have 200 (222, 250, 274, 296, 320, 344, 368, 390) sts on needles.

LEFT FRONT

Continue with stitches before first marker only and at the same time keep working the front increases as established on every 4th row after first 3 sts 11 (10, 8, 8, 7, 7, 5, 5, 4) more times, until you have worked the increases a total of 19 (19, 19, 20, 20, 21, 21, 22, 22) times. Work two rows back and forth in St st in MC. Then attach CC and begin striping: two rows in CC, two rows in MC.

Continue until the sleeve opening measures 5.5 (5.75, 6.25, 6.5, 7.25, 8, 8.75, 9.25, 10.5)” / 13.5 (14.5, 15.5, 16.5, 18, 20, 22, 24, 26) cm on the shoulder end. End with a WS row and cut yarns. Place sts on holder or waste yarn.

UPPER BACK

Continue with back stitches, stitches between the markers, only. On first row place the single shoulder seam stitches, the single reverse St sts next to markers on each end, on holders. Work two rows back and forth in St st in MC. Then attach CC and begin striping: two rows in CC, two rows in MC.

Continue until the sleeve opening measures 5.5 (5.75, 6.25, 6.5, 7.25, 8, 8.75, 9.25, 10.5)” / 13.5 (14.5, 15.5, 16.5, 18, 20, 22, 24, 26) cm on the shoulder end. End with a WS row and cut yarns. Place sts on holder or waste yarn.

RIGHT FRONT

Continue with stitches before first marker only and at the same time keep working the front increases as established on every 4th row after first 3 sts 11 (10, 8, 8, 7, 7, 5, 5, 4) more times, until you have worked the increases a total of 19 (19, 19, 20, 20, 21, 21, 22, 22) times. Work two rows back and forth in St st in MC. Then attach CC and begin striping: two rows in CC, two rows in MC.

Continue until the sleeve opening measures 5.5 (5.75, 6.25, 6.5, 7.25, 8, 8.75, 9.25, 10.5)” / 13.5 (14.5, 15.5, 16.5, 18, 20, 22, 24, 26) cm on the shoulder end. End with a WS row and cut MC and CC. Place sts on holder or waste yarn.

JOIN FOR LOWER BODY

Joining rnd (RS, attach the right colour to keep striping continuous): Knit left front stitches, knit back stitches, knit right front stitches.

You should have 220 (240, 264, 288, 308, 332, 348, 376, 396) sts on needles for body.

LOWER BODY

Continue even in St st and keep striping as established until the body measures 14” / 35 cm from underarm, ending with CC stripe. Cut CC and continue with MC only.

Change to US 2 / 2.75 mm needles. Work 2” / 5 cm of 1 x 1 ribbing. BO body sts on next RS round in ribbing.

SLEEVES

Using US 4 / 3.5 mm needles and keeping the striping continuous, attach the right colour to underarm. Pick up and knit 30 (32, 34, 36, 40, 44, 48, 53, 57) sts up to shoulder, knit the single shoulder stitch from holder and pick up and knit 29 (31, 33, 35, 39, 43, 47, 52, 56) sts down to centre of underarm. 60 (64, 68, 72, 80, 88, 96, 106, 114) sts on needles.

Continue even in St st and keep striping as established until the sleeve measures 2" / 5 cm from underarm.

Begin sleeve decreases
Dec rnd: K2, ssk, knit to last 4 sts, k2tog, k2.

Repeat the decrease round on every 12th (12th, 12th, 10th, 10th, 10th, 8th, 8th, 8th) round 5 (6, 6, 6, 7, 8, 9, 10, 11) more times, keeping striping continuous. 48 (50, 54, 58, 64, 70, 76, 84, 90) sts on needles.

Continue striping until the sleeve measures 14" / 35 cm. End with MC stripe. Cut CC and continue with MC only.

Change to US 2 / 2.75 mm needles. Work 2" / 5 cm in 1 x 1 ribbing. BO sleeve sts on next round in ribbing.

BUTTONBAND

Using US 2 / 2.75 mm needles and MC, CO 13 sts.

Next row (WS): (P1, k1) 6 times, p1.

Starting at right bottom front corner start attaching the buttonband to the front edge row by row as follows. Note: If you have trouble picking up and knitting the stitches from the front edge as you go, pick them up on a spare needle beforehand; pick the stitches up in ratio 1 st / 2 rows.

Row 1 (RS): (K1, p1) 6 times, sl1 kwise, pick up and knit 1 stitch from the edge of the body, pass the slipped st over.
Row 2 (WS): (P1, k1) 6 times, p1.

Rep the last 2 rows up the right front edge until the buttonband measures 1" / 2.5 cm. Work first buttonhole.

Buttonhole row (RS): (K1, p1) 3 times, yo, k2tog, (p1, k1) twice, sl1 kwise, pick up and knit 1 stitch from the edge of the body, pass the slipped st over.

Repeat the buttonhole row every 3.5" / 9 cm for 3 more times. Keep working the buttonband as established up the right front to the CO edge of the neck, across back of the neck and finally down left front. BO buttonband sts in ribbing.

FINISHING

Weave in all yarn ends and block the cardigan to measurements using your preferred method. Sew on buttons.

If I look into that old mirror, what will I see? Do I see the world as it is or do I see something else? Like an old fairy tale, this shawl plays with the idea of reversed or mirrored stripes. The sequence is simple, but the outcome is very graphic and striking. It captures the modern day in its every shift.

The KAARNA shawl is worked from the top down, but in two parts – attaching the two halves together as you go. Joining the second half to the first simultaneously will keep the centre seam stretchier than seaming it afterwards.

SIZES

1 (2)

Shown in size 2.

FINISHED MEASUREMENTS

Wingspan: 78 (98)" / 200 (248) cm.
Depth: 13 (16)" / 33 (40) cm.

MATERIALS

Yarn: 1 (1) cone of Nurtured Fine by Julie Asselin (100% fine wool, 780 yds / 708 m – 112 g), colourway Fonte as main colour (MC). Or approx. 620 (700) yds / 567 (640) m of light fingering weight yarn.

1 (1) cone of Nurtured Fine by Julie Asselin (100% fine wool, 780 yds / 708 m – 112 g), colourway Naturel as contrasting colour (CC). Or approx. 620 (700) yds / 567 (640) m of light fingering weight yarn.

Needles: US 4 / 3.5 mm 32" / 80 cm circular needles, or size needed to obtain the gauge.

Notions: Tapestry needle and blocking aids.

GAUGE

20 sts x 44 rows to 4" / 10 cm on US 4 / 3.5 mm needles in garter stitch, after blocking.

DIRECTIONS

FIRST HALF

Using MC and circular needles, CO 5 sts.
ROW 1 (RS): K2, k1fbf, k2.
ROW 2 (WS): K2, k1fb, k4.
ROW 3 (RS): Knit to last 4 sts, k1fbf, k3.
ROW 4: K2, k1fb, knit to end.

Repeat rows 3 and 4, 8 more times.

35 sts on needles.

Cut MC and attach CC.

Work rows 3 and 4, 10 times.

65 sts on needles.

Continue as established repeating rows 3 and 4, 10 times, first in MC then in CC. Continue until you have 4 (5) stripes in each colour for the half.

245 (305) sts on needles.

BO all sts loosely on next row (RS).

SECOND HALF

Using CC and circular needles, CO 5 sts. Note: If you struggle with picking up stitches from the vertical edge as you go, you can also pick up the stitches on spare needle in ratio 1 stitch every 2 rows before starting the second half.

ROW 1 (RS): K2, k1fbf, k1, sl 1, pick up and knit one from first row of first half, pass the slipped stitch over.
ROW 2: Knit to last 4 sts, k1fb, k3.
ROW 3 (RS): K2, k1fbf, knit to last st and slip knitwise, pick up and knit 1 st from the next row of first half, pass the slipped st over.
ROW 4: Knit to last 4 sts, k1fb, k3.

Repeat rows 3 and 4, 8 more times.

35 sts on needles.

Cut CC and attach MC.

Work rows 3 and 4, 10 times.

65 sts on needles.

Continue as established repeating rows 3 and 4, 10 times, first in CC then in MC. Continue until you have 4 (5) stripes in each colour for the half.

245 (305) sts on needles.

BO all sts loosely on next row (RS).

FINISHING

Weave in all yarn ends carefully. Block the shawl to measurements using wires and pins.

Maire

The morning of the first snow is always so exciting. It covers the grey landscape in brilliant white and small diamonds. That cold morning makes the everyday seem magical.

The MAIRE dress plays with that strong contrast between the white snow and the dark ground. It has generous ease, a straight body and an unusual shoulder construction. The dress starts with the upper back worked as a raglan sweater back, but then stitches are picked up for the shoulders and joined for the upper front.

SIZES

1 (2, 3, 4, 5, 6, 7, 8, 9)

Shown in size 3. Recommended ease: 8" / 20 cm of positive ease.

FINISHED MEASUREMENTS

Bust Circumference: 40 (44, 48, 52, 56, 60, 64, 68, 72)" / 100 (110, 120, 130, 140, 150, 160, 170, 180) cm.
Upper Arm Circumference: 15 (16, 17, 18, 19, 20, 21, 22, 22)" / 38 (40, 42, 46, 48, 50, 54, 56, 56) cm.
Armhole Depth: 7.5 (8, 8.5, 9, 9.5, 10, 10.5, 11, 11)" / 19 (20, 21, 23, 24, 25, 27, 28, 28) cm.
Body Length (from underarm) (all sizes): 26" / 65 cm.
Sleeve Length (from underarm) (all sizes): 20" / 50 cm.
Cuff Circumference: 7 (7.5, 8, 9, 10, 11, 12, 13, 14.5)" / 18 (19, 20, 24, 25, 28, 32, 34, 36) cm.

MATERIALS

Yarn: 5 (5, 6, 6, 7, 7, 8, 8, 9) skeins of Shelter by Brooklyn Tweed (100% wool, 140 yds / 128 m – 50 g), colourway Fossil as main colour (MC). Or approx. 560 (640, 720, 820, 900, 970, 1050, 1115, 1180) yds / 510 (580, 660, 750, 820, 890, 960, 1020, 1080) m of worsted weight yarn.

5 (5, 6, 6, 7, 7, 8, 8, 9) skeins of Shelter by Brooklyn Tweed (100% wool, 140 yds / 128 m – 50 g), colourway Cast Iron as contrasting colour (CC). Or approx. 550 (620, 700, 760, 820, 900, 985, 1060, 1140) yds / 500 (570, 650, 690, 750, 820, 900, 970, 1040) m of worsted weight yarn.

Needles: US 6 / 4 mm 32" / 80 cm circular needles and US 8 / 5 mm 32" / 80 cm circular needles and DPNs for sleeves in each size if not using magic loop method for short circumference knitting, or size needed to obtain the gauge.

Notions: Stitch markers, stitch holders or waste yarn, tapestry needle.

GAUGE

18 sts x 26 rows to 4" / 10 cm on US 8 / 5 mm needles in Stockinette stitch, after blocking.

NOTES

Stripe sequence: Work 35 rows/rounds of each colour for the block stripes throughout the dress. For hem and cuff ribbing, continue with the last colour worked.

DIRECTIONS

UPPER BACK

Using US 8 / 5 mm needles and MC, CO 32 (32, 32, 34, 34, 36, 36, 36) sts. Do not join. Purl to first row, and then begin increases.

Row 1 (RS): K4, m1l, knit to last 4 sts, m1r, k4.
Row 2 (WS): Purl to end.

Repeat rows 1 and 2, 25 (27, 31, 35, 39, 43, 47, 51, 55) more times and remember to change the colour after every 35 rows as you will throughout the dress. After all back increases you should have 84 (88, 96, 106, 114, 122, 132, 140, 148) sts on needles. Cut yarn and place stitches on holder.

RIGHT SHOULDER

Using US 8 / 5 mm needles and MC, starting from the corner of live stitches on holder, pick up and knit 30 (32, 36, 42, 46, 50, 56, 60, 64) sts along the increase edge to the corner of back of the neck. Purl to end. Shape the shoulder with short rows and decreases.

Row 1 (RS): K3, w&t.
Row 2 (WS): P to end.
Row 3 (RS): Knit to previous wrapped stitch, PUW, k1, w&t.
Row 4 (WS): P to end.
Row 5 (RS): K4, ssk, knit to previous wrapped stitch, PUW, k1, w&t.
Row 6 (WS): P to end.

Repeat rows 3–6, 5 (6, 7, 8, 9, 10, 11, 12, 12) more times. Knit to end on next row and pick up the last wrap. Continue even and work decreases 3 (2, 1, 2, 1, –, 1, –, –) more time(s) on every 4th row as established.

Decrease row (RS): K4, ssk, knit to end.
When the piece measures 3" / 8 cm from back of the neck corner, begin front increases.

Increase row (RS): Knit to last 4 stitches, m1l, k4.
Repeat the increase row 4 more times every second row (every RS row). End with last increase row (RS). Cut yarn.

LEFT SHOULDER

Using US 8 / 5 mm needles and MC, starting from the corner of back of the neck, pick up and knit 30 (32, 36, 42, 46, 50, 56, 60, 64) sts from the increase edge. Shape the shoulder with short rows and decreases.

Row 1 (WS): P3, w&t.
Row 2 (RS): K to end.
Row 3 (WS): Purl to previous wrapped stitch, PUW, p1, w&t.
Row 4 (RS): K to end.
Row 5 (WS): Purl to previous wrapped stitch, PUW, p1, w&t.
Row 6 (RS): K to last 6 sts, k2tog, k4.

Repeat rows 3–6, 5 (6, 7, 8, 9, 10, 11, 12, 12) more times. Purl to end on next row and pick up the last wrap. Continue even and work decreases 3 (2, 1, 2, 1, –, 1, –, –) more time(s) on every 4th row as established.

Decrease row (RS): K to last 6 sts, k2tog, k4.
When the piece measures 3" / 8 cm from back of the neck corner, begin front increases.

Increase row (RS): K4, m1r, knit to end.
Repeat the increase row 4 more times every second row (every RS row). Keep yarn attached.

UPPER FRONT

Join shoulders on next row (WS): Purl left shoulder stitches, CO 32 (32, 32, 34, 34, 34, 36, 36, 36) sts using backwards-loop cast-on, purl right front stitches. You should have 84 (88, 96, 106, 114, 122, 132, 140, 148) sts on needles. Work even in St st and remember to change colour so it matches the back. To make sure you are changing at the correct time, fold the front over the back. Continue until the front matches the back piece, end with a WS row.

Join for lower body
Joining rnd (RS): PM for beginning of rnd, knit front stitches, CO 6 (12, 12, 12, 12, 14, 12, 14, 14) sts using backwards loop CO, knit back stitches and CO 6 (12, 12, 12, 12, 14, 12, 14, 14) sts using backwards loop CO.

You should have 180 (200, 216, 236, 252, 272, 288, 308, 324) sts on needles for body.

LOWER BODY

Continue even in St st and change colour after every 35 rounds as established until the body measures 24" / 60 cm from underarm.

Change to US 6 / 4 mm needles. Work 2" / 5 cm of 1 x 1 ribbing. BO body sts on next round in 1 x 1 ribbing.

SLEEVES

Using US 8 / 5 mm needles, attach MC to centre of underarm cast-on edge. Pick up and knit 3 (6, 6, 6, 6, 7, 6, 7, 7) sts from underarm CO edge, pick up and knit 62 (60, 64, 68, 74, 78, 82, 86, 86) sts along sleeve opening to underarm cast on edge, pick up and knit 3 (6, 6, 6, 6, 7, 6, 7, 7) sts to centre of underarm. You should have 68 (72, 76, 80, 86, 90, 94, 100, 100) sts on needles.

Continue even in St st and change colour after every 35 rounds as established until the sleeve measures 2" / 5 cm from underarm. Begin sleeve decreases.

Dec rnd: K2, ssk, knit to last 4 sts, k2tog, k2.

Repeat the decrease round on every 8th round 8 (8, 9, 9, 9, 10, 10, 10, 10) more times. 50 (54, 56, 60, 66, 68, 72, 78, 78) sts on needles. Continue striping as established until the sleeve measures 16" / 40 cm.

Change to US 6 / 4 mm needles. Work 2" / 5 cm in 1 x 1 ribbing. BO sleeve sts on next round in ribbing.

COLLAR

Using US 6 / 4 mm needles and MC, with RS facing, attach yarn to back of the neck cast-on edge. Pick up and knit 32 (32, 32, 34, 34, 34, 36, 36, 36) sts from the back of the neck, pick up and knit 24 sts (all sizes) from left shoulder, pick up and knit 32 (32, 32, 34, 34, 34, 36, 36, 36) sts from front of the neck and pick up and knit 24 sts (all sizes) from right shoulder. PM for beginning of round. 112 (112, 112, 116, 116, 116, 120, 120, 120) sts on needles.

Work 10 rounds in 1 x 1 ribbing. BO collar stitches in ribbing on next rnd.

FINISHING

Weave in all yarn ends and block the dress to measurements using your preferred method.

Varpu

Finding comfort inside your home is a privilege that you do not always think about before something stirs the balance. Whenever I have moved house, I have always struggled with the change. Where would that sense of safety come from next?

The VARPU shawl has a traditional triangle shape, but plays with textures, short rows and two-coloured brioche after the single-coloured beginning. Subtle heathery colours make this shawl and the stripes very delicate and understated. It is something you will enjoy knitting and wearing. This shawl resembles that safe place, that comfort, something you can carry with you wherever you go.

SIZE

One Size

FINISHED MEASUREMENTS

Wingspan: 72" / 184 cm.
Depth at centre spine: 36" / 92 cm.

MATERIALS

Yarn: 4 skeins of Rustic Heather Sport by Lichen and Lace (100% Canadian wool, 215 yds / 196 m – 56 g), colourway Snow as main colour (MC). Or approx. 790 yds / 720 m of sport weight yarn.

3 skeins of Rustic Heather Sport by Lichen and Lace (100% Canadian wool, 215 yds / 196 m – 56 g), colourway Rose as first contrasting colour (CC1). Or approx. 580 yds / 530 m of sport weight yarn.

1 skein of Rustic Heather Sport by Lichen and Lace (100% Canadian wool, 215 yds / 196 m – 56 g), colourway Pollen as second contrasting colour (CC2). Or approx. 100 yds / 90 m of sport weight yarn.

Needles: US 6 / 4 mm 32" / 80 cm circular needles.

Notions: Tapestry needle, stitch markers (including one locking stitch marker).

GAUGE

18 sts x 36 rows to 4" / 10 cm on US 6 / 4 mm needles in garter stitch, after blocking.

SPECIAL ABBREVIATIONS AND TECHNIQUES

I-Cord BO
Continue with the attached i-cord edging. RS: *K3, slip the next stich knitwise, knit the next stitch (first of the live stitches of bottom edge). Pass the 4th stitch over the knitted edge stitch. Slide the just knitted 4 stitches back onto left needle.* Repeat *–* until you have worked all bottom edge stitches and reach the other end of the i-cord (8 stitches remain). Graft the ends of the i-cord together.

BRK: Brioche knit. Knit slipped stitch together with its yarn over.

BRKYOBRK: Brioche knit, yarn over, brioche knit into the same stitch. (2 sts inc'd)
BRP: Brioche purl. Purl slipped stitch together with its yarn over.

SL1YO: With yarn in front slip 1 stitch purlwise, yarn over.

DIRECTIONS

GARTER STITCH BEGINNING, COLOUR 1

Using circular needles and MC, provisionally CO 4 stitches. Note: You will first work a bit of i-cord to begin your shawl. Work 7 rows of i-cord: *Knit the stitches and slide or slip them back onto the left tip of the needle*, repeat *–* 6 times. Slide/slip the stitches back onto the left tip, knit 4 sts, pick up and knit 5 stitches from the vertical edge of your i-cord (1 stitch/row and the extra rows for the i-cord ends), place the provisionally cast on stitches onto the left tip of your circular and knit those 4 stitches. You should have 13 stitches on needles, 4 on each end for i-cord finishing and 5 picked up from the length of the i-cord.

SET-UP ROW (MC, WS): Slip the first 4 sts wyif, k3, PM, k2, slip the last 4 sts wyif.
ROW 1 (RS): K4, k1fb, knit to 1 st before marker, k1fb, SM, k1fb, knit to last 6 sts, k1fb, knit to end.
ROW 2 (WS): Slip the first 4 sts wyif, knit to last 4 sts, slip the last 4 sts wyif.

Repeat the last 2 rows 40 more times. 177 sts total.

FIRST BRIOCHE SECTION

Continue with MC and attach CC1.
SET-UP ROW (MC, RS): K4, sl1yo, (k1, yo, k1) into one st, *sl1yo, k1*, rep *–* to 2 sts before marker, sl1yo, (k1, yo, k1) into one st, SM, sl1yo, (k1, yo, k1) into one st, sl1yo, *k1, sl1yo*, rep *–* to last 6 sts, (k1, yo, k1) into one st, sl1yo, k4.
SET-UP ROW (CC1, RS): Slide sts back to left tip to continue on RS. K4, *brp, sl1yo*, rep *–* to m, SM, brp, *sl1yo, brp*, rep *–* to last 4 sts, k4.
ROW 1 (MC, WS): Slip the first 4 sts wyif, *sl1yo, brp*, rep *–* to 1 st before marker, sl1yo, SM, *brp, sl1yo*, rep *–* to last 4 sts, slip the last 4 sts wyif.
ROW 2 (CC1, WS): Slide sts back to left tip to continue on WS. Slip the first 4 sts wyif, *brk, sl1yo*, repeat *–* to 1 st before marker, brk, SM, *sl1yo, brk*, repeat *–* to last 4 sts, slip the last 4 sts wyif.
ROW 3 (MC, RS): K4, sl1yo, brkyobrk, *sl1yo, brk*, rep *–* to 2 sts before marker, sl1yo, brkyobrk, SM, sl1yo, brkyobrk, sl1yo, *brk, sl1yo*, rep *–* to last 6 sts, brkyobrk, sl1yo, k4.
ROW 4 (CC1, RS): Slide sts back to left tip to continue on RS. K4, *brp, sl1yo*, rep *–* to m, SM, brp, *sl1yo, brp*, rep *–* to last 4 sts, k4.

Repeat last 4 rows 8 more times, then work rows 1 and 2 once more. 80 sts inc'd, 257 sts total. Cut MC.

FIRST GARTER STITCH SHORT ROWS

Attach CC1 and continue with CC1 only.
ROW 1 (RS, CC1): K4, k1fb, knit to 1 st before marker, k1fb, SM, k1fb, knit to last 6 sts, k1fb, knit to end.
ROW 2 (WS, CC1): Slip the first 4 sts wyif, knit to last 4 sts, slip the last 4 sts wyif.
ROW 3: K4, k1fb, knit to 1 st before marker, k1fb, SM, k1fb, knit to last 28 sts, w&t.
ROW 4: Knit to last 4 sts, slip the last 4 sts wyif.
ROW 5: K4, k1fb, knit to 1 st before marker, k1fb, SM, k1fb, knit to 1 st before previous wrapped st, w&t.
ROW 6: Knit to last 4 sts, slip the last 4 sts wyif.

Repeat the last 2 rows 6 more times. 285 sts.

Attach CC2. Note: You will knit all the way to end across all sts on the first RS row; there's no need to pick up the wraps as they will blend in garter stitch nicely.
ROW 1 (RS, CC2): K4, k1fb, knit to 1 st before marker, k1fb, SM, k1fb, knit to last 6 sts, k1fb, knit to end.
ROW 2 (WS): Slip the first 4 sts wyif, k25, w&t. Place a locking stitch marker to this first wrapped st to indicate the correct turning point for later short rows.
ROW 3: Knit to last 6 sts, k1fb, knit to end.
ROW 4: Slip the first 4 sts wyif, knit until you have knitted the previous wrapped st, w&t.

Repeat the last 2 rows 6 more times. 296 sts.

ROW 5: Knit to last 6 sts, k1fb, knit to end.
ROW 6: Slip the first 4 sts wyif, knit to last 4 sts, slip the last 4 sts wyif.

Cut CC2. 40 sts inc'd, 297 sts.

SECOND BRIOCHE SECTION

Attach MC, keep CC1 attached.
SET-UP ROW (MC, RS): K4, sl1yo, (k1, yo, k1) into one st, *sl1yo, k1*, rep *–* to 2 sts before marker, sl1yo, (k1, yo, k1) into one st, SM, sl1yo, (k1, yo, k1) into one st, sl1yo, *k1, sl1yo*, rep *–* to last 6 sts, (k1, yo, k1) into one st, sl1yo, k4.
SET-UP ROW (CC1, RS): Slide sts back to left tip to continue

on RS. K4, *brp, sl1yo*, rep *–* to marker, SM, brp, *sl1yo, brp*, rep *–* to last 4 sts, k4.

ROW 1 (MC, WS): Slip the first 4 sts wyif, *sl1yo, brp*, rep *–* to 1 st before marker, sl1yo, SM, *brp, sl1yo*, rep *–* to last 4 sts, slip the last 4 sts wyif.

ROW 2 (CC1, WS): Slide sts back to left tip to continue on WS. Slip the first 4 sts wyif, *brk, sl1yo*, rep *–* to 1 st before marker, brk, SM, *sl1yo, brk*, rep *–* to last 4 sts, slip the last 4 sts wyif.

ROW 3 (MC, RS): K4, sl1yo, brkyobrk, *sl1yo, brk*, rep *–* to 2 sts before marker, sl1yo, brkyobrk, SM, sl1yo, brkyobrk, sl1yo, *brk, sl1yo*, rep *–* to last 6 sts, brkyobrk, sl1yo, k4.

ROW 4 (CC1, RS): Slide sts back to left tip to continue on RS. K4, *brp, sl1yo*, rep *–* to marker, SM, brp, *sl1yo, brp*, rep *–* to last 4 sts, k4.

Repeat last 4 rows 8 more times, then work rows 1 and 2 once more.

80 sts inc'd, 377 sts total. Cut MC.

SECOND GARTER STITCH SHORT ROWS

Attach CC1 and continue with CC1 only.

ROW 1 (RS, CC1): K4, k1fb, knit to 1 st before marker, k1fb, SM, k1fb, knit to last 6 sts, k1fb, knit to end.

ROW 2 (WS, CC1): Slip the first 4 sts wyif, knit to last 4 sts, slip the last 4 sts wyif.

ROW 3: K4, k1fb, knit to 1 st before marker, k1fb, SM, k1fb, knit until you have knitted the stitch marked by the locking stitch marker, w&t.

ROW 4: Knit to last 4 sts, slip the last 4 sts wyif.

ROW 5: K4, k1fb, knit to 1 st before marker, k1fb, SM, k1fb, knit to 1 st before previous wrapped st, w&t.

ROW 6: Knit to last 4 sts, slip the last 4 sts wyif.

Repeat the last 2 rows 6 more times. 405 sts.

Attach CC2. Note: You will knit all the way to end across all sts on the first RS row; there's no need to pick up the wraps as they will blend in garter stitch nicely.

ROW 1 (RS, CC2): K4, k1fb, knit to 1 st before marker, k1fb, SM, k1fb, knit to last 6 sts, k1fb, knit to end.

ROW 2 (WS): Slip the first 4 sts wyif, knit to the stitch marked by the locking stitch marker, w&t.

ROW 3: Knit to last 6 sts, k1fb, knit to end.

ROW 4: Slip the first 4 sts wyif, knit until you have knitted the

previous wrapped stitch, w&t.

Repeat the last 2 rows 6 more times. 416 sts.

ROW 5: Knit to last 6 sts, k1fb, knit to end.

ROW 6: Slip the first 4 sts wyif, knit to last 4 sts, slip the last 4 sts wyif.

Cut CC2. 40 sts inc'd, 417 sts.

LAST BRIOCHE SECTION

Continue with MC and attach CC1.

SET-UP ROW (MC, RS): K4, sl1yo, (k1, yo, k1) into one st, *sl1yo, k1*, rep *–* to 2 sts before marker, sl1yo, (k1, yo, k1) into one st, SM, sl1yo, (k1, yo, k1) into one st, sl1yo,*k1, sl1yo*, rep *–* to last 6 sts, (k1, yo, k1) into one st, sl1yo, k4.

SET-UP ROW (CC1, RS): Slide sts back to left tip to continue on RS. K4, *brp, sl1yo*, rep *–* to m, SM, brp, *sl1yo, brp*, rep *–* to last 4 sts, k4.

ROW 1 (MC, WS): Slip the first 4 sts wyif, *sl1yo, brp*, rep *–* to 1 st before marker, sl1yo, SM, *brp, sl1yo*, rep *–* to last 4 sts, slip the last 4 sts wyif.

ROW 2 (CC1, WS): Slide sts back to left tip to continue on WS. Slip the first 4 sts wyif, *brk, sl1yo*, slip the last 4 sts wyif.

ROW 3 (MC, RS): K4, sl1yo, brkyobrk, *sl1yo, brk*, rep *–* to 2 sts before marker, sl1yo, brkyobrk, SM, sl1yo, brkyobrk, sl1yo, *brk, sl1yo*, rep *–* to last 6 sts, brkyobrk, sl1yo, k4.

ROW 4 (CC1, RS): Slide sts back to left tip to continue on RS. K4, *brp, sl1yo*, rep *–* to m, SM, brp, *sl1yo, brp*, rep *–* to last 4 sts, k4.

Repeat last 4 rows 3 more times, then work rows 1 and 2 once more.

40 sts inc'd, 457 sts total. Cut CC1. BO all sts using i-cord BO using MC.

FINISHING

Weave in all yarn ends. Block the shawl to measurements using wires and pins.

Venny

Summer! Oh, how I long to see you again, my dear old friend. The long days of never-ending sunlight, a warm breeze on my face, the touch of grass under my toes. Those are the days I live for!

VENNY is a round yoke sweater, perfectly capturing that feeling of summer ease; the time when there is no rush, no haste. The delicate colours of the rustic and soulful wool remind me of the late summer evenings and of that hazy light I so love.

SIZES

1 (2, 3, 4, 5, 6, 7, 8, 9)

Shown in size 3. Recommended ease: 4–6” / 10–15 cm of positive ease.

FINISHED MEASUREMENTS

Bust Circumference: 36 (40, 44, 48, 52, 56, 60, 64, 68)” / 90 (100, 110, 120, 130, 140, 150, 160, 170) cm.
Upper Arm Circumference: 10.5 (11.5, 12.5, 14, 15.5, 17, 18.5, 20, 22)” / 27 (29, 31, 35, 39, 42, 46, 50, 55) cm.
Yoke Depth: 7 (7.5, 8, 9, 9.5, 10, 10.5, 11, 11.5)” / 18 (19, 20, 22, 24, 25, 26, 27, 28) cm.
Body Length (from underarm) (all sizes): 14” / 36 cm.
Sleeve Length (from underarm) (all sizes): 18” / 45 cm.
Cuff Circumference: 7 (7.5, 8, 9, 10, 11, 12, 13, 14.5)” / 18 (19, 20, 24, 25, 28, 30, 32, 28) cm.

MATERIALS

Yarn: 4 (4, 4, 5, 5, 5, 6, 6, 7) skeins of BFL/Masham DK by Woolly Mammoth Fibre Company (75% BFL, 25% Masham – 100% wool, 260 yds / 240 m – 100 g), colourway Natural as main colour (MC). Or approx. 840 (920, 1000, 1090, 1180, 1300, 1430, 1570, 1675) yds / 770 (840, 920, 1000, 1080, 1190, 1310, 1440, 1530) m of DK weight yarn.

1 (1, 1, 1, 2, 2, 2, 2, 2) skein(s) of BFL/ Masham DK by Woolly Mammoth Fibre Company (75% BFL, 25% Masham – 100% wool, 260 yds / 240 m – 100 g), colourway Peony as contrasting colour (CC). Or approx. 200 (210, 230, 250, 285, 320, 350, 380, 420) yds / 180 (190, 210, 230, 260, 290, 320, 350, 380) m of DK weight yarn.

Needles: US 4 / 3.5 mm 32” / 80 cm circular needles and US 8 / 5 mm 32” / 80 cm circular needles and DPNs for sleeves in each size if not using magic loop method for short circumference knitting, or size needed to obtain the gauge.

Notions: Stitch markers, stitch holders or waste yarn, tapestry needle, row counter.

GAUGE

18 sts x 24 rows to 4” / 10 cm on US 8 / 5 mm needles in Stockinette stitch, after blocking.

SPECIAL ABBREVIATIONS

Sk2po: Slip 1 stitch as if to knit, knit next 2 stitches together, pass slipped stitch over. (2 sts dec'd)
K3tog: Knit 3 stitches together. (2 sts dec'd)

STITCH PATTERN

Lace
Lace, worked over 12 rows
Row 1 (RS): *Yo, k1, ssk, k3, k2tog, k1, yo, p1*, repeat *–* once.
Row 2 (RS): *K1, yo, k1, ssk, k1, k2tog, k1, yo, k1, p1*, repeat *–* once.
Row 3: K2, yo, k1, sk2po, k1, yo, k2, p1, k2, yo, k1, k3tog, k1, yo, k2, p1.
Row 4: K3, yo, k1, ssk, k3, p1, k3, k2tog, k1, yo, k3, p1.
Row 5: K4, yo, k1, ssk, k2, p1, k2, k2tog, k1, yo, k4, p1.
Row 6: K5, yo, k1, ssk, k1, p1, k1, k2tog, k1, yo, k5, p1.
Row 7: *Yo, k1, ssk, k3, k2tog, k1, yo, p1*, repeat *–* once.
Row 8: K1, yo, k1, ssk, k1, k2tog, k1, yo, k1, p1*, repeat *–* once.
Row 9: K2, yo, k1, k3tog, k1, yo, k2, p1, k2, yo, k1, sk2po, k1, yo, k2, p1.
Row 10: K3, k2tog, k1, yo, k3, p1, k3, yo, k1, ssk, k3, p1.
Row 11: K2, k2tog, k1, yo, k4, p1, k4, yo, k1, ssk, k2, p1.
Row 12: K1, k2tog, k1, yo, k5, p1, k5, yo, k1, ssk, k1, p1.

NOTE

Read the chart from bottom to top and from right to left.

DIRECTIONS

COLLAR

Using US 4 / 3.5 mm needles and MC, CO 96 sts (all sizes) using a long-tail CO. Carefully join in the round and PM to indicate the beginning of round. Work 10 rounds in 1 x 1 ribbing.

YOKE

Change to US 8 / 5 mm needles and increase on first round.
Inc rnd 1: *K2, m1l*, repeat *–* to end of rnd. 144 sts.

Shape the back of the neck using short rows as follows.
Row 1 (RS): SM, k20, w&t.
Row 2 (WS): Purl to marker, SM, p20, w&t.
Row 3: Knit to marker, SM, knit to previous wrapped st, PUW, k3, w&t.
Row 4: Purl to marker, SM, p to previous wrapped st, PUW, p3, w&t.

Repeat last 2 rows twice more.

Work 1.5" / 4 cm in St st.

Inc rnd 2: *K3 (3, 3, 2, 2, 2, 2, 2), m1l*, repeat *–* to end of rnd.

192 (192, 192, 216, 216, 216, 216, 216, 216) sts.

Knit 2 more rnds in MC. Attach CC and begin striping: work 2 rnds in CC, 4 rnds in MC. When the piece measures 2.5" / 6 cm from previous increase rnd, work another set of increases.
Inc rnd 3: *K4 (4, 4, 3, 3, 3, 3, 3, 3), m1l*, repeat *–* to end of rnd.

240 (240, 240, 288, 288, 288, 288, 288, 288) sts.

Sizes – (–, –, –, –, 6, 7, 8, 9) only
When the piece measures 2.5" / 6 cm from previous increase rnd, work another set of increases.

Inc rnd 4: *Knit – (–, –, –, –, 4, 4, 3, 2), m1l*, repeat *–* to end of rnd.

– (–, –, –, –, 360, 360, 384, 432) sts.

All sizes
After all yoke increases continue even in St st and keep striping as established until the yoke measures 7 (7.5, 8, 9, 9.5, 10, 10.5, 11, 11.5)" / 18 (19, 20, 22, 24, 25, 26, 27, 28) cm from the front.

Divide for body and sleeves
Dividing rnd: SM, knit 38 (40, 40, 47, 48, 58, 58, 62, 68), place the next 44 (41, 40, 50, 49, 65, 65, 69, 81) sts on holder for sleeve, CO 4 (11, 20, 14, 21, 11, 19, 21, 18) sts using backwards loop CO, knit 76 (79, 80, 94, 95, 115, 115, 123, 135), place the next 44 (41, 40, 50, 49, 65, 65, 69, 81) sts on holder for sleeve, CO 4 (11, 20, 14, 21, 11, 19, 21, 18) sts using backwards loop CO, knit 38 (39, 40, 47, 47, 58, 58, 61, 67) to end of rnd.

You should have 160 (180, 200, 216, 232, 252, 268, 288, 306) sts on needles and 44 (41, 40, 50, 49, 65, 65, 69, 81) sts on each holder for sleeves.

BODY

Continue even in St st and keep striping as established until the body measures 7" / 18 cm from underarm, ending with CC stripe. Cut CC.

Knit one round in MC and increase on following round for lace: SM, *knit – (–, –, 54, 29, 31, 22, 24, 21), m1l*, repeat *–* – (–, –, 3, 7, 7, 11, 11, 13) time(s), k to end if necessary in your size.

160 (180, 200, 220, 240, 260, 280, 300, 320) sts on needles.

Begin lace: Work rows 1–12 of lace twice across all stitches [working a total of 8 (9, 10, 11, 12, 13, 14, 15, 16) repeats of lace pattern on each round].

Change US 4 / 3.5 mm needles. Work 14 rounds of 1 x 1 ribbing. BO body sts on next round in ribbing.

SLEEVES

Place the sleeve stitches from holder to US 8 / 5 mm needles. Keeping the striping continuous, attach the right colour to center of underarm cast on sts, and pick up and knit 2 (6, 9, 7, 11, 6, 10, 11, 10) sts to stitches on needle, knit 44 (41, 40, 50, 49, 65, 65, 69, 81) sleeve stitches, pick up and knit 2 (5, 9, 7, 10, 5, 9, 10, 9) sts to center of underarm. 48 (52, 58, 64, 70, 76, 84, 90, 100) sts on needles.

Continue even in St st and keep striping as established until the sleeve measures 3" / 8 cm from underarm. Begin sleeve decreases.

Dec rnd: K2, ssk, knit to last 4 sts, k2tog, k2.

Repeat the decrease round on every 12th (12th, 8th, 8th, 8th, 8th, 8th, 6th, 6th) round 5 (6, 7, 8, 8, 9, 10, 11, 12) more times, keeping striping continuous. 36 (38, 42, 46, 52, 56, 62, 66, 74) sts on needles.

Continue striping until the sleeve measures 16" / 40 cm.

Change to US 4 / 3.5 mm needles. Work 2" / 5 cm in 1 x 1 ribbing. BO sleeve sts on next round in ribbing.

FINISHING

Weave in all yarn ends and block the sweater to measurements using your preferred method.

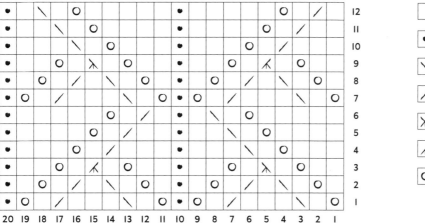

Symbol	Meaning
□	Knit
•	Purl
\	Ssk
/	K2tog
⋋	Sk2po
⋌	K3tog
O	Yo

Playing with stripes, the ELLEN wrap is all about the garter stitch spiced up with easy short rows. This shawl resembles two arrow heads, pointing at each other, but the shape is still a symmetric rectangle.

The Ellen wrap is worked sideways in one piece. Choose colours with enough contrast to highlight the striking look of this long and lovely wrap.

SIZE
One Size

FINISHED MEASUREMENTS

Length: 84" / 214 cm.
Depth: 18" / 46 cm.

MATERIALS

Yarn: 3 skeins of Cashmerino DK by Fru Valborg (80% SW Merino, 10% cashmere, 230 yds / 212 m – 100 g), colourway Petrol as main colour (MC). Or approx. 660 yds / 600 m of DK weight yarn.

2 skeins of Cashmerino DK by Fru Valborg (80% SW Merino, 10% cashmere, 230 yds / 212 m – 100 g), colourway Emmy Lou as contrasting colour (CC). Or approx. 420 yds / 385 m of DK weight yarn.

Needles: US 7 / 4.5 mm 32" / 80 cm circular needles, or size needed to obtain the gauge.

Notions: Tapestry needle, stitch markers.

GAUGE

16 sts x 32 rows to 4" / 10 cm on US 7 / 4.5 mm needles in garter stitch, after blocking.

SPECIAL TECHNIQUE

I-cord BO
Continue with the attached i-cord edging. RS: *K3, slip the next stitch kwise, knit the next stitch (first of the live stitches of bottom edge). Pass the 4th stitch over the knitted edge stitch. Slide the just knitted 4 sts back onto left needle.* Repeat *–* until you have worked all bottom edge stitches and reach the other end of the i-cord (8 sts remain). Graft the two ends of the i-cord together using Kitchener stitch.

DIRECTIONS

SET-UP

Using circular needles and MC, provisionally CO 4 stitches. Note: You will first work a bit of i-cord to begin your stole. Work 10 rows of i-cord: *Knit the stitches and slide/slip them back onto the left tip of the needle*, repeat *–* 9 times. Slide/slip the stitches back onto the left tip, knit 4 sts, pick up and knit 7 stitches from the vertical edge of your i-cord (1 stitch/row and the extra rows for the i-cord ends), place the provisionally cast on stitches onto the left tip of your circular and knit those 4 stitches.

You should have 15 stitches on needles, 4 on each end for i-cord finishing and 7 sts picked up from length of the i-cord.

SET-UP ROW (MC, WS): Slip the first 4 sts wyif, knit to last 4 sts, slip the last 4 sts wyif.
ROW 1 (MC, RS): K4, k1fb, k1fb, PM, k2, k1fb, k1fb, k5. 19 sts.
ROW 2 (MC, WS): Slip the first 4 sts wyif, knit to last 4 sts, slip the last 4 sts wyif.
ROW 3: K4, k1fb, knit to 1 st before marker, k1fb, SM, k2, k1fb, knit to last 6 sts, k1fb, k5.
ROW 4: Slip the first 4 sts wyif, knit to last 4 sts, slip the last 4 sts wyif.

Rep rows 3 and 4, 19 more times.

99 sts on needles.

STRIPES

Attach CC and continue striping with MC and CC as follows.
ROW 1 (MC, RS): K4, k2tog, knit to 1 st before marker, k1fb, SM, k2, k1fb, knit to last 6 sts, ssk, k4.
ROW 2 (MC, WS): Slip the first 4 sts wyif, knit to last 4 sts, slip the last 4 sts wyif.
ROW 3 (CC, RS): K4, k2tog, knit to 1 st before marker, k1fb, SM, k2, k1fb, knit to last 6 sts, ssk, k4.
ROW 4 (CC, WS): Slip the first 4 sts wyif, knit to last 4 sts, slip the last 4 sts wyif.
Rep rows 1–4, 14 more times.

99 sts on needles; you have worked 15 stripes in CC.

Work rows 1 and 2 once more (MC).

SHORT ROW STRIPES

Continue with short row stripes in MC and CC as follows. Note: There's no need to pick up the wraps as they will blend in garter stitch nicely.
ROW 1 (CC, RS): K4, k2tog, knit to 1 st before marker, k1fb, SM, k2, w&t.
ROW 2 (CC, WS): Knit to last 4 sts, slip the last 4 sts wyif.
ROW 3 (MC, RS): K4, k2tog, knit to 1 st before marker, k1fb, SM, k2, k1fb, knit to last 6 sts, ssk, k4.
ROW 4 (MC, WS): Slip the first 4 sts wyif, knit to 2 sts before marker, w&t.
ROW 5 (MC, RS): K1fb, knit to last 6 sts, ssk, k4.
ROW 6 (MC, WS): Slip the first 4 sts wyif, knit to last 4 sts, slip the last 4 sts wyif.

Rep rows 1–6, 37 more times.

Still 99 sts on needles; you have worked 38 halfway stripes in CC.

SHORT ROWS IN CC

Cut MC. Continue with short row stripes in CC as follows. Note: You will first work the short rows on first half of the stitches, then on the second half. After these two sets of short rows, the live stitches should be even and horizontal. Then you will work another set of short rows on the second half and lastly work a second set on the first half of the wrap. There's no need to pick up the wraps as they will blend in garter stitch nicely. After all the short rows the shape of the live stitches is reversed compared to the first half of the wrap.

ROW 1 (CC, RS): K4, k2tog, knit to 1 st before marker, k1fb, SM, k2, k1fb, knit to last 6 sts, ssk, k4.
ROW 2 (CC, WS): Slip the first 4 sts wyif, knit to last 4 sts, slip the last 4 sts wyif.
ROW 3 (CC, RS): K4, w&t.
ROW 4 (CC, WS): Slip the last 4 sts wyif.
ROWS 5 AND 7: K4, knit until you have knitted the previous wrapped st, w&t.
ROWS 6 AND 8: Knit to last 4 sts, slip the last 4 sts wyif.
ROW 9: K4, k2tog, knit until you have knitted the previous wrapped st, w&t.
ROW 10: Knit to last 4 sts, slip the last 4 sts wyif.

Rep rows 5–10, 13 more times, until you only have 1 unwrapped st before the marker.

ROW 11 (RS): K4, k2tog, knit to 1 st before marker, k1fb, SM, k2, k1fb, knit to last 6 sts, ssk, k4.

ROW 12 (WS): Slip the first 4 sts wyif, w&t.

ROWS 13 AND 15: Knit to end.

ROWS 14 AND 16: Slip the first 4 sts wyif, knit until you have knitted the previous wrapped st, w&t.

ROW 17: Knit to last 6 sts, ssk, k4.

ROW 18 (WS): Slip the first 4 sts wyif, knit until you have knitted the previous wrapped st, w&t.

Rep rows 13–18, 13 more times, until you have 4 sts unwrapped before the marker (WS).

ROW 19 (RS): Knit to end.

ROW 20 (WS): Slip the first 4 sts wyif, knit to 4 sts before marker, w&t.

ROWS 21 AND 23: Knit to end.

ROWS 22 AND 24: Slip the first 4 sts wyif, knit to 1 st before the previous wrapped st, w&t.

ROW 25: Knit to last 5 sts, k1fb, k4.

ROW 26: Slip the first 4 sts wyif, knit to 1 st before the previous wrapped st, w&t.

Rep rows 21–26, 13 more times.

ROW 27 (RS): Knit to end.

ROW 28 (WS): Slip the first 4 sts wyif, knit to last 4 sts, slip the last 4 sts wyif.

ROW 29: Knit to 1 st before marker, w&t.

ROW 30: Knit to last 4 sts, slip the last 4 sts wyif.

ROWS 31 AND 33: Knit to 1 st before the previous wrapped st, w&t.

ROWS 32 AND 34: Knit to last 4 sts, slip the last 4 sts wyif.

ROW 35: K4, k1fb, knit to 1 st before the previous wrapped st, w&t.

ROW 36: Knit to last 4 sts, slip the last 4 sts wyif.

Rep rows 31–36, 13 more times, until you only have 1 st unwrapped before the marker.

After all short row sets you should again have 99 sts on needles.

STRIPES

Attach MC and continue striping with CC and MC as follows.

SET-UP ROW (MC, RS): K4, k1fb, knit to 1 st before marker, slip the next st on right needle, RM, slip the previous st back onto left needle, k2tog, PM, k1, ssk, knit to last 6 sts, k1fb, k5.

SET-UP ROW 2 (MC, WS): Slip the first 4 sts wyif, knit to last 4 sts, slip the last 4 sts wyif.

ROW 1 (CC, RS): K4, k1fb, knit to 2 sts before marker, k2tog, SM, k1, ssk, knit to last 6 sts, k1fb, k5.

ROW 2 (CC, WS): Slip the first 4 sts wyif, knit to last 4 sts, slip the last 4 sts wyif.

ROW 3 (MC, RS): K4, k1fb, knit to 2 sts before marker, k2tog, SM, k1, ssk, knit to last 6 sts, k1fb, k5.

ROW 4 (MC, WS): Slip the first 4 sts wyif, knit to last 4 sts, slip the last 4 sts wyif.

Rep rows 1–4, 14 more times.

99 sts on needle; you have worked 15 stripes in CC.

FINAL PART IN MC

Cut CC and continue with MC.

ROW 1 (MC, RS): K4, k2tog, knit to 2 sts before marker, k2tog, SM, k1, ssk, knit to last 6 sts, ssk, k4.

ROW 2 (MC, WS): Slip the first 4 sts wyif, knit to last 4 sts, slip the last 4 sts wyif.

Rep rows 1 and 2, 20 more times, until you have 15 sts on needle. BO remaining stitches using i-cord bind-off.

FINISHING

Weave in all yarn ends carefully and block the wrap to measurements using wires and pins.

Anni

The ANNI socks are inspired by Swedish polkagris candy all the way down to the colours I chose. Sweet knee high socks are a fun in-between project that will keep your feet happy. These socks are a small but not too small project with plenty of easy knitting.

The socks are worked from the toe up. You will reverse the colours for the second sock to make them extra playful and also to make the most out of your yarn. Keep careful notes on the number of the stripes worked to help you keep the striping reversed, especially before starting the gusset increases on the first sock.

SIZES

1 (2)

Shown in size 1.

FINISHED MEASUREMENTS

Calf circumference at widest part: 10 (11)" / 25.5 (28) cm.
Foot circumference: 8 (9)" / 20 (22.5) cm.
Height from Heel to Top of Cuff (unfolded) (both sizes): 20" / 50 cm.

MATERIALS

Yarn: 1 (1) skein of Mondim by Retrosaria Rosa Pomar (100% wool, 421 yds / 385 m – 100 g), colourway 111 (red) as main colour (MC). Or approx. 385 (415) yds / 355 (380) m of fingering weight yarn.

1 (1) skein of Mondim by Retrosaria Rosa Pomar (100% wool, 421 yds / 385 m – 100 g), colourway 100 (white) as contrasting colour (CC). Or approx. 385 (415) yds / 355 (380) m of fingering weight yarn.

Needles: US 1.5 / 2.5 mm and US 0 / 2 mm circular needles or DPNs in same sizes.

Notions: Stitch marker, tapestry needle.

GAUGE

30 sts and 36 rnds to 4" / 10 cm on US 1.5 / 2.5 mm needles in Stockinette stitch, after blocking.

DIRECTIONS

TOE

Using larger needles and MC (first sock) / CC (second sock), CO 24 (24) sts using Judy's Magic CO or provisional CO and divide sts evenly on needles: 6 (6) sts on each DPN or 12 (12) sts on each end of the circular needle. Note: The first half of stitches is for the sole of the sock.

Knit one rnd then begin increases as follows:
Rnd 1 (RS): K1, m1l, knit to 1 sts before the centre of stitches, m1r, k2, m1l, knit to 1 st before end, m1R, k1.
Rnd 2 (RS): Knit to e nd.

Repeat rnds 1 and 2, 9 (11) more times.
You should have 60 (68) sts on needles.

FOOT

Knit 3 more rnds in MC (first sock) / CC (second sock).

Begin striping as follows: First sock – Knit 2 rnds in CC, knit 2 rnds in MC / Second sock – Knit 2 rnds in MC, knit 2 rnds in CC. Work striping as established until the sock measures approx. 4.5" / 12 cm shorter than the desired final length of the foot. Remember to take a note of the number of stripes worked, so you will work the same amount for the second sock. Begin gusset increases. Keep striping as established.

Rnd 1 (RS): K1, m1l, knit to 1 sts before the centre of stitches, m1r, k to end.
Rnd 2 (RS): K to end.

Repeat rnds 1 and 2, 14 (16) more times.

30 (34) sts increased; you should have 60 (68) sts for sole and 30 (34) sts for instep on the needles.

HEEL

Begin short rows for the heel turn. Note: Work in the colour of the next row of stripes would be.
Short row 1 (RS): Knit 15 (17), PM, knit 29 (33), w&t.
Short row 2 (WS): Purl to 1 st before marker, w&t.
Short row 3 (RS): Knit to 2 sts before the previous wrapped st, w&t.

Short row 4 (WS): Purl to 2 sts before the previous wrapped st, w&t.

Repeat short rows 3 and 4 until you have 6 sts between the wrapped sts. Continue with heel flap.

Row 1 (RS): Knit and at the same time pick up all wraps you come across (ssk the wrap with the wrapped st, making sure the wrap stays on WS) until the last wrapped stitch, work a sssk with the wrapped stitch, wrap and the following stitch. Turn work.
Row 2 (WS): Purl and at the same time pick up all wraps you come across (p2tog the wraps with the wrapped st) until the last wrapped stitch, work a p3tog with the wrapped stitch, wrap and the following stitch and remove the marker. Turn work.
Row 3 (RS): Slip 1 purlwise, *k1, sl 1 purlwise*, repeat *–* to last st before the gap (the previous turning point), ssk, turn work.
Row 4 (WS): Slip 1 purlwise, purl to last st before the gap (the previous turning point), p2tog, turn work.

Repeat rows 3 and 4 until all sts increased for the gusset are decreased.
60 (68) sts on needles.

LEG

Work in st st and keep striping as established for 4" / 10 cm. Then begin calf increases.
Set-up rnd: K15 (17), PM, knit to end of rnd.
Increase rnd: K to 2 sts before m, m1l, k2, SM, k2, m1r, knit to end.

Repeat increase rnd on every 8th rnd 7 more times.
You should have 76 (84) sts on needles.

Work in St st and keep striping until the sock measures 17" / 42 cm from the heel, ending with MC stripe (first sock) / CC stripe (second sock). Cut CC (first sock) / MC (second sock). Change to smaller needles. Work in 2 x 2 ribbing for 3" / 8 cm. BO sts loosely in ribbing.

FINISHING

If you used provisional CO, graft toe stitches with Kitchener st. Weave in all yarn ends. Block the socks to measurements using your preferred method.

Helle

Like waves on a lakeshore or gathering storm clouds on the
horizon, this top allows the volume of the fabric to work its magic.
This minimal top is all about the movement of the pleats with
the simple striping being the focal point.

HELLE is worked sideways, starting with the front, and then
continuing with the back. For little finishing details, you will
work a bit of reverse Stockinette to the neck and sleeve openings.
To keep the hem from curling, you will add a bit of ribbing.

SIZES

1 (2, 3, 4, 5, 6, 7, 8, 9)

Shown in size 3. Recommended ease: 2–4" / 5–10 cm of positive ease. Note: The ease does not include the ease from pleats.

FINISHED MEASUREMENTS

High Bust Circumference (ease from pleats not included): 34 (38, 42, 46, 50, 54, 58, 62, 64)" / 85 (95, 105, 115, 125, 135, 145, 155, 165) cm.
Width of back of the neck: 7.25 (7.25, 7.25, 7.5, 7.5, 8, 8, 8, 8)" / 18 (18, 18, 19, 19, 20, 20, 20, 20) cm.
Shoulder width: 3.5 (3.5, 4, 4, 4.5, 4.75, 5.25, 5.5, 6)" / 9 (9, 10, 10, 11, 12, 13, 14, 15) cm.
Depth from shoulder to underarm: 7 (7.5, 8, 8.25, 8.75, 9, 9.5, 10, 10.5)" / 18 (19, 20, 21, 22, 23, 24, 25, 26) cm.
Body Length (from underarm to hem): 18.5 (18.5, 18.5, 18.5, 19, 19, 19.5, 19.5, 19.5)" / 46 (46, 46, 46, 47.5, 47.5, 48.5, 48.5, 48.5) cm.

MATERIALS

Yarn: 6 (6, 7, 7, 8, 8, 9, 9) skeins of Lyonesse 4-ply by Blacker Yarns (50% Falkland wool, 50% linen, 190 yds / 175 m – 50 g), colourway Sapphire as main colour (MC). Or approx. 1080 (1180, 1270, 1370, 1460, 1540, 1620, 1700, 1780) yds / 990 (1080, 1160, 1250, 1340, 1400, 1480, 1550, 1630) m of fingering weight yarn.

2 (2, 2, 3, 3, 4, 4, 4) skeins of Lyonesse 4-ply by Blacker Yarns (50% Falkland wool, 50% linen, 190 yds / 175 m – 50 g), colourway Moonstone as contrasting colour (CC). Or approx. 280 (330, 370, 430, 490, 550, 610, 680, 740) yds / 260 (300, 340, 390, 450, 505, 560, 620, 680) m of fingering weight yarn.

Needles: US 4 / 3.5 mm and US 2 / 3 mm 32" / 80 cm circular needles.

Notions: Stitch markers, including one locking stitch marker, spare circular needle, tapestry needle.

GAUGE

24 sts x 34 rows to 4" / 10 cm on US 4 / 3.5 mm needles in Stockinette stitch, after blocking.

NOTES

Work the stripes as follows: 8 rows/rounds of MC followed by 2 rows of CC. Note that the pleats don't follow this pattern, but are always worked into the MC part of the striping.

DIRECTIONS

FRONT

Using MC and larger needles, provisionally CO 111 (111, 111, 111, 114, 114, 117, 117, 117) sts. On RS, work the first 8 sts in 1 x 1 ribbing and continue in St st to end. On WS, work in St st to last 8 sts and work in 1 x 1 ribbing to end. After 2 rows, begin striping: 8 rows of MC followed by 2 rows of CC. Work as established until the piece measures 1.25 (2.5, 2.75, 3.5, 4, 4.5, 5.25, 5.25, 6.5)" / 3 (6, 7, 9, 10, 11, 13, 13, 16) cm, and then begin underarm shaping as follows (RS): Work to last 5 sts, m1r, knit to end. Repeat shaping on every RS row 4 more times. On next RS row increase for upper body: Work to last 5 sts, m1r, knit to end, CO 36 (39, 42, 44, 46, 49, 51, 54, 57) sts using backwards loop cast-on.

You should have a total of 153 (156, 159, 161, 166, 169, 174, 177, 180) sts on needles.

On next MC section, work the first pleat: Work the first 4 rows of MC. Then work only the first 121 (123, 125, 125, 127, 129, 131, 133, 135) sts and turn. Work to end on WS. Repeat the two rows working only the first 121 (123, 125, 125, 127, 129, 131, 133, 135) sts 5 more times. (Partly row worked 12 times total). Work to end in MC for the next 4 rows. Note: You will have a gaping hole in your work where the pleat is, you will sew them to the WS in the finishing. Continue with striping as established and work a pleat for each MC section until you bind off stitches for the end of upper body.

When the shoulder piece measures 3.5 (3.5, 4, 4, 4.5, 4.75, 5.25, 5.5, 6)" / 9 (9, 10, 10, 11, 12, 13, 14, 15) cm, decrease on next WS row for the neck edge (WS): BO the first 18 (20, 22, 22, 24, 24, 26, 26, 28) sts, work to end. Note: Keep working the stripes and pleats as established. Decrease on the following four RS rows: Work to last 5 sts, k2tog, k3.

Work even as established until the straight top edge measures 5.25 (5.25, 5.25, 5.5, 5.5, 6, 6, 6, 6)" / 13 (13, 13, 14, 14, 15, 15, 15, 15) cm. Note: If your row gauge differs, keep working until your whole neck opening measures 7.25 (7.25, 7.25, 7.5, 7.5, 8, 8, 8, 8)" / 18 (18, 18, 19, 19, 20, 20, 20, 20) cm from the BO including the upcoming 8 rows for the increases. Begin neck increases, making sure your stripes are centered before starting the increases. Start the increases the closest you can to the measurements, either shorter or slightly longer if necessary. Increase on the following four RS rows: Work to last 4 sts, m1r, k4. Then increase for the neck: Work to end and CO 18 (20, 22, 22, 24, 24, 26, 26, 28) sts using backwards loop cast-on.

Work even as established working stripes and pleats, until the shoulder piece measures 3.5 (3.5, 4, 4, 4.5, 4.75, 5.25, 5.5, 6)" / 9 (9, 10, 10, 11, 12, 13, 14, 15) cm. Then decrease on next WS row for the upper body (WS): BO the first 36 (39, 42, 44, 46, 49, 51, 54, 57) sts, work to end. Note: Keep working the stripes as established. Pleats are now completed. Decrease on the following six RS rows: Work to last 5 sts, k2tog, k3.

You should have a total of 111 (111, 111, 111, 114, 114, 117, 117, 117) sts on needles.

Work as established 1.25 (2.5, 2.75, 3.5, 4, 4.5, 5.25, 5.25, 6.5)" / 3 (6, 7, 9, 10, 11, 13, 13, 16) cm more – or measure by folding the front in half to keep striping symmetrical.

BACK

Place a locking stitch marker to indicate the beginning of the back. Using MC, continue with the stitches on needles and work the back. On RS, work the first 8 sts in 1 x 1 ribbing and continue in St st to end. On WS, work in St st to last 8 sts and work in 1 x 1 ribbing to end. After 2 rows, begin striping: 8 rows of MC followed by 2 rows of CC.

Work as established until the piece measures 1.25 (2.5, 2.75, 3.5, 4, 4.5, 5.25, 5.25, 6.5)" / 3 (6, 7, 9, 10, 11, 13, 13, 16) cm, and then begin underarm shaping as follows (RS): Work to last 5 sts, m1r, knit to end. Repeat shaping on every RS row 4 more times. On next RS row increase for upper body: Work to last 5 sts, m1r, knit to end, CO 36 (39, 42, 44, 46, 49, 51, 54, 57) sts using backwards loop cast-on.

You should have a total of 153 (156, 159, 161, 166, 169, 174, 177, 180) sts on needles.

When the shoulder piece measures 3.5 (3.5, 4, 4, 4.5, 4.75, 5.25, 5.5, 6)" / 9 (9, 10, 10, 11, 12, 13, 14, 15) cm, decrease on next WS row for the neck edge (WS): BO the first 6 (6, 8, 8, 10, 10, 10, 12, 12) sts, work to end. Note: Keep working the striping as established. Decrease on the following four RS rows: Work to last 5 sts, k2tog, k3.

Work even as established until the straight top edge measures 5.25 (5.25, 5.25, 5.5, 5.5, 6, 6, 6, 6)" / 13 (13, 13, 14, 14, 15,

15, 15, 15) cm. Note: If your row gauge differs, keep working until your whole neck opening measures 7.25 (7.25, 7.25, 7.5, 7.5, 8, 8, 8, 8)" / 18 (18, 18, 19, 19, 20, 20, 20, 20) cm from the BO including the upcoming 8 rows for the increases. Begin neck increases, making sure your stripes are centred before starting the increases. Start the increases closest you can to the measurements, either shorter or slightly longer if necessary. Increase on the following four RS rows: Work to last 4 sts, m1r, k4. Then increase for the neck: Work to end and CO 6 (6, 8, 8, 10, 10, 10, 12, 12) sts using backwards loop cast-on.

Work even as established working stripes, until the shoulder piece measures 3.5 (3.5, 4, 4, 4.5, 4.75, 5.25, 5.5, 6)" / 9 (9, 10, 10, 11, 12, 13, 14, 15) cm. Then decrease on next WS row for the upper body (WS): BO the first 36 (39, 42, 44, 46, 49, 51, 54, 57) sts, work to end. Decrease on the following six RS rows: Work to last 5 sts, k2tog, k3.

You should have a total of 111 (111, 111, 111, 114, 114, 117, 117, 117) sts on needles.

Work as established until the piece measures 1.25 (2.5, 2.75, 3.5, 4, 4.5, 5.25, 5.25, 6.5)" / 3 (6, 7, 9, 10, 11, 13, 13, 16) cm – or measure by folding the back in half to keep striping symmetrical.

Release the provisional CO edge to a spare needle. Fold the sweater with WS facing and hold the two needles parallel. BO the live sts on needles and the CO edge together using MC and a three-needle BO.

FINISHING

Seam the shoulders together. Sew the pleats to WS as follows: fold the pleats toward the center on each side of the front, pin them down and sew the top edge of each fold to the front in a straight line. If you have an odd number of pleats, fold the center pleat flat (pleat points to each direction).

NECK

Using MC and smaller needles, starting from the top of the right shoulder, pick up and knit 54 (54, 56, 58, 58, 60, 60, 64, 64) sts from the back of the neck, 24 (24, 26, 26, 28, 28, 30, 32, 34) sts down the left vertical edge of the front, 30 (30, 30, 32, 32, 34, 34, 34) sts from the horizontal part of front neck edge, 24 (24, 26, 26, 28, 28, 30, 32, 34) sts up the right vertical

edge of the neck to the starting point. PM and join in round. You should have 132 (132, 138, 142, 146, 150, 154, 162, 166) sts on needles.

Work 7 rounds in reverse St st. BO all sts loosely in reverse St st.

SLEEVES

Pick up and knit 55 (62, 69, 78, 84, 90, 98, 104, 114) sts from centre of underarm to top of shoulder and 55 (62, 69, 78, 84, 90, 98, 104, 114) sts down to center of underarm. PM and join in round.

You should have 110 (124, 138, 156, 168, 180, 196, 208, 228) sts on needles.

Work 7 rounds in reverse St st. BO all sts loosely in reverse St st.

Weave in all yarn ends carefully and block the top to measurements using your preferred method.

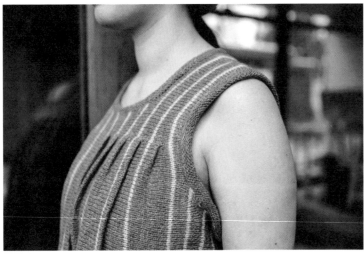

Maija

I'm always longing to see the sea. I love to sit on the pier, watching the sails being hoisted and listening to the seagulls sing. That is the place where I feel calm.

MAIJA is a new take on the classic sailor sweater, this time worked in crisp colours with plenty of positive ease. Maija is ever so stylish and very comfortable to wear.

SIZES

1 (2, 3, 4, 5, 6, 7, 8, 9)

Shown in size 3. Recommended ease: 8" / 20 cm of positive ease.

FINISHED MEASUREMENTS

Bust circumference: 40 (44, 48, 52, 56, 60, 64, 68, 72)" / 100 (110, 120, 130, 140, 150, 160, 170, 180) cm.
Upper Arm Circumference: 11 (12, 13, 14, 15, 16.5, 18, 19.5, 21)" / 28 (30, 33, 36, 38, 41, 45, 49, 53) cm.
Armhole Depth: 7 (8, 8.5, 9, 9.5, 10, 10.5, 11, 11.5)" / 18 (20, 22, 23, 25, 26, 28, 29) cm.
Body Length (from underarm) (all sizes): 20" / 50 cm.
Sleeve Length (from underarm) (all sizes): 18" / 45 cm.
Cuff Circumference: 7 (7.5, 8, 9, 10, 11, 12, 13, 14.5)" / 18 (19, 20, 24, 25, 28, 32, 34, 36) cm.

MATERIALS

Yarn: 2 (2, 2, 3, 3, 3, 3, 4, 4) skeins of Merino Sport by La Bien Aimée (100% SW Merino, 355 yds / 325 m – 100 g), colourway Winter as main colour (MC). Or approx. 520 (600, 690, 790, 880, 960, 1050, 1140, 1230) yds / 480 (550, 630, 720, 800, 880, 960, 1040, 1120) m of sport weight yarn.

2 (2, 2, 3, 3, 3, 3, 4, 4) skeins of Merino Sport by La Bien Aimée (100% SW Merino, 355 yds / 325 m – 100 g), colourway Mariniere Bleue as first contrasting colour (CC1). Or approx. 500 (570, 660, 740, 830, 920, 1010, 1105, 1215) yds / 460 (520, 600, 680, 760, 840, 920, 1010, 1110) m of sport weight yarn.

1 (1, 1, 1, 1, 2, 2, 2, 2) skeins of Merino Sport by La Bien Aimée (100% SW Merino, 355 yds / 325 m – 100 g), colourway La Bien Aimée Yellow as second contrasting colour (CC2). Or approx. 200 (240, 285, 320, 350, 395, 440, 480, 525) yds / 180 (220, 260, 290, 320, 360, 400, 440, 480) m of sport weight yarn.

Needles: US 1.5 / 2.5 mm 32" / 80 cm circular needles and US 2.5 / 3 mm 32" / 80 cm circular needles and DPNs for sleeves in each size if not using magic loop method for short circumference knitting, or size needed to obtain the gauge.

Notions: Stitch markers, stitch holders or waste yarn, tapestry needle.

GAUGE

26 sts x 36 rows to 4" / 10 cm on US 2.5 / 3 mm needles in Stockinette stitch, after blocking.

DIRECTIONS

SHOULDER PIECES

Using US 2.5 / 3 mm needles and MC, CO 52 (52, 56, 56, 60, 60, 64, 64, 68) sts. Do not join. Work 8 rows in MC, the attach CC1 and begin striping: Two rows in CC1, four rows in MC. After 3 CC stripes, begin decreases.

Decrease row (RS): K5, k2tog, knit to last 7 sts, ssk, knit to end.

Repeat the decrease row 3 (3, 3, 3, 4, 4, 5, 5, 5) more times.

44 (44, 48, 48, 50, 50, 52, 52, 56) sts on needles.

Continue striping as established until the piece measures 5 (5.5, 6, 6.25, 6.75, 7.25, 7.75, 7.75, 8)" / 12 (14, 15, 16, 17, 18, 19, 19, 20) cm. Cut each yarn and place stitches on holder.

Work second piece similarly.

BODY

Next you will pick up stitches from the long edges of the shoulder pieces and cast on stitches for each front and back of the neck and for each underarm.

Using US 2.5 / 3 mm needles and MC, with RS facing and starting at the corner of stitches on holder, pick up and knit 31 (35, 40, 44, 45, 48, 50, 50, 53) sts from the long edge of the first shoulder piece, CO 40 (40, 40, 40, 44, 44, 44, 48, 48) sts for front of the neck using backwards loop CO, pick up and knit 31 (35, 40, 44, 45, 48, 50, 50, 53) sts from the long edge of the second shoulder piece (starting from the corner of CO edge and working down to sts on holder), CO 28 (34, 36, 42, 48, 56, 64, 74, 80) sts for underarm using backwards loop CO, pick up and knit 31 (35, 40, 44, 45, 48, 50, 50, 53) sts from the long edge of the second shoulder piece (starting from the corner of sts on holder and working down to CO edge), CO 40 (40, 40, 40, 44, 44, 44, 48, 48) sts for back of the neck using backwards loop CO, pick up and knit 31 (35, 40, 44, 45, 48, 50, 50, 53) sts from the long edge of the second shoulder piece (starting from the corner of CO edge and working down to sts on holder), CO 28 (34, 36, 42, 48, 56, 64, 74, 80) sts for underarm using backwards loop CO. Join in round and PM for beginning of round. You should have 260 (288, 312, 340, 364, 392, 416, 444, 468) sts on needles.

Continue even in St st and keep striping as established until the body measures 13" / 33 cm from underarm, ending with a CC1 stripe. Cut MC and attach CC2. From now on work striping as follows: 4 rounds in CC2 and 2 rounds in CC1. Continue striping 4" / 10 cm more. Then cut CC2 and continue with CC1 only. Work 1" / 2 cm in St st.

Change to US 1.5 / 2.5 mm needles. Divide the stitches in half for split hem as follows.
Next row (RS): SM, knit to centre of underarm stitches, tw.
Next row (WS): Knit to marker, RM, knit 14 (17, 18, 21, 24, 28, 32, 37, 40), tw.

Work 2" / 5 cm in garter st. BO front stitches on next row.

With RS facing, attach CC1 to back stitches. Work 2" / 5 cm in garter st. BO back stitches on next row.

SLEEVES

Using US 2.5 / 3 mm needles, attach MC to centre of underarm cast on edge. Pick up and knit 14 (17, 18, 21, 24, 29, 32, 37, 40) sts from underarm CO edge to stitches on holder, knit 44 (44, 48, 48, 50, 50, 52, 52, 56) sts from holder and pick up and knit 14 (17, 18, 21, 24, 29, 32, 37, 40) sts to centre of underarm. PM to indicate beginning of round. You should have 72 (78, 84, 90, 98, 108, 116, 126, 136) sts on needles.

Continue even in St st and keep striping as established (four rounds in MC, two rounds in CC1) until the sleeve measures 3" / 8 cm from underarm. Begin sleeve decreases.

Dec rnd: K2, ssk, knit to last 4 sts, k2tog, k2.

Repeat the decrease round on every 10th (8th, 8th, 8th, 8th, 6th, 6th, 6th, 6th) round 8 (9, 9, 10, 10, 11, 11, 12, 13) more times, keeping striping continuous. 54 (58, 64, 68, 76, 84, 94, 100, 108) sts on needles.

Continue striping until the sleeve measures 10" / 25 cm. End with CC1 stripe. Cut MC and attach CC2.

From now on work striping as follows: 4 rounds in CC2 and 2 rounds in CC1. Continue striping and working remaining decreases 6" / 15 cm more, ending with CC1 stripe. Then cut CC2 and continue with CC1 only.

Change to US 1.5 / 2.5 mm needles and work 2" / 5 cm in garter st.
BO sleeve stitches on next round.

COLLAR

Using US 1.5 / 2.5 mm needles with RS facing, attach MC to left corner
of back of the neck. Pick up and knit 52 (52, 56, 56, 60, 60, 64, 64, 68)
sts from left shoulder edge, PM, pick up and knit 40 (40, 40, 40, 44, 44,
44, 48, 48) sts from front of the neck, PM, pick up and knit 52 (52, 56,
56, 60, 60, 64, 64, 68) sts from right shoulder edge, PM and pick up and
knit 40 (40, 40, 40, 44, 44, 44, 48, 48) sts from back of the neck. PM to
indicate beginning of round. You should have 184 (184, 192, 192, 208,
208, 216, 224, 232) sts on needles.

Rnd 1 (RS): *SM, k2tog, knit to 2 sts before marker, ssk*, repeat *–*
3 more times.
Rnd 2: Purl to end.

Repeat rounds 1–2, 5 (5, 5, 5, 6, 6, 6, 7, 7) more times. Knit one more
round and BO all sts on next round.

FINISHING

Weave in all yarn ends and block the sweater to measurements using
your preferred method.

Alli

This shawl is inspired by the ripples on water and a new crescent moon on the horizon. ALLI is worked in one piece, starting as a regular crescent shaped shawl. With short rows it changes to a more asymmetric crescent, with a slightly deeper curve making it even more wearable. Thanks to twisted ribbing, this shawl is fully reversible – you can hardly see a difference.

SIZE

One Size

FINISHED MEASUREMENTS

Wingspan: 80" / 204 cm.
Depth (at deepest point): 17" / 43 cm.

MATERIALS

Yarn: 3 skeins of Cottage Merino by Walk Collection (100% SW Merino, 400 yds / 360 m – 100 g), colourway Peach Pop. Or approx. 1090 yds / 1000 m of fingering weight yarn.

Needles: US 4 / 3.5 mm 32" / 80 cm circular needles.

Notions: Stitch marker, tapestry needle.

GAUGE

22 sts x 44 rows to 4" / 10 cm on US 4 / 3.5 mm needles in garter stitch, after blocking.

DIRECTIONS

GARTER STITCH BEGINNING

Using circular needles, CO 5 stitches.

Set-up row (WS): K1, k1fb, k1fb, k2.
Row 1 (RS): K1, k1fbf, knit to last 3 sts, k1fbf, k2.
Row 2 (WS): K1, k1fb, knit to last 3 sts, k1fb, k2.

Repeat rows 1 and 2, 14 more times. You should have 97 sts on needles.

Work first increases as follows:
Increase row (RS): K1, k1fbf, *k2, yo*, repeat *–* 44 more times, k2, k1fbf, k2.
Work the next row as row 2.

You should have 148 sts on needles.

TWISTED RIBBING

Row 3 (RS): K1, k1fb, *k1tbl, p1tbl*, repeat *–* to last 4 sts, k1tbl, k1fb, k2.
Row 4 (WS): K1, k1fb, *p1tbl, k1tbl*, repeat *–* to last 4 sts, p1tbl, k1fb, k2.

Repeat rows 3 and 4, 5 more times (you have now 12 rows of twisted ribbing).

Next 2 rows: K1, k1fb, knit to last 3 sts, k1fb, k2.

You should have 176 sts on needles. 28 sts inc'd.

FIRST SHORT ROWS

Row 5 (RS): K1, k1fb, k10, turn work.
Row 6 (WS): Knit to last 3 sts, k1fb, k2.
Row 7 (RS): K1, k1fb, knit to previous turning point, yo, k10, turn work.
Row 8 (WS): Knit to last 3 sts, k1fb, k2.

Repeat rows 7 and 8, 14 more times.

Knit to end on next row (RS): K1, k1fb, knit to previous turning point, yo, knit to last 3 sts, k1fb, k2.
Next row (WS): K1, k1fb, knit to last 3 sts, k1fb, k2.

You should have 228 sts on needles.

Work a set of increases as follows:
Increase row (RS): K1, k1fb, k4, *k8, yo*, repeat *–* 25 more times, k11, k1fb, k2.

Work the next row as row 2.

You should have 258 sts on needles.

TWISTED RIBBING

Work as previously. You should have 286 sts on needles.

SECOND SHORT ROWS

Row 5 (RS): K1, k1fb, k10, turn work.
Row 6 (WS): Knit to last 3 sts, k1fb, k2.
Row 7 (RS): K1, k1fb, knit to previous turning point, yo, k10, turn work.
Row 8 (WS): Knit to last 3 sts, k1fb, k2.

Repeat rows 7 and 8, 26 more times.

Knit to end on next row (RS): K1, k1fb, knit to previous turning point, yo, k1fb, k2.
Next row (WS): K1, k1fb, knit to last 3 sts, k1fb, k2.

You should have 374 sts on needles.

Work a set of increases as follows:
Increase row (RS): K1, k1fb, k11, yo, *k12, yo*, repeat *–* 28 more times, k10, k1fb, k2.
Work the next row as row 2.

You should have 408 sts on needles.

TWISTED RIBBING

Work as previously.
You should have 436 sts on needles.

THIRD SHORT ROWS

Row 5 (RS): K1, k1fb, k10, turn work.
Row 6 (WS): Knit to last 3 sts, k1fb, k2.

Row 7 (RS): K1, k1fb, knit to previous turning point, yo, k10, turn work.
Row 8 (WS): Knit to last 3 sts, k1fb, k2.

Repeat rows 7 and 8, 40 more times.

Knit to end on next row (RS): K1, k1fb, knit to previous turning point, yo, knit to last 3 sts, k1fb, k2.
Next row (WS): K1, k1fb, knit to last 3 sts, k1fb, k2.

You should have 566 sts on needles.

BO all sts on next row loosely.

FINISHING

Weave in all yarn ends carefully and block the shawl to measurements using your preferred method.

Maria

I am often longing for those bright summer mornings, the ones when the sun has barely set before it gets up again. They give me hope of everything growing and renewing. That very moment is the inspiration behind this triangular shawl. Soothing garter stitch is paired with yummy stripes and rustic wool.

MARIA is worked sideways and in a diagonal, attaching the second and third part as you go. You will first knit the sideways triangle with stripes, then the second triangle in colour 2 diagonally from the bottom corner of the striped part. Lastly, the third triangle is worked from the centre top of the full shawl.

SIZES

One Size

FINISHED MEASUREMENTS

Wingspan: 76" / 192 cm.
Depth: 34" / 86 cm.

MATERIALS

Yarn: 1 skein of No. 4 by G-Uld (75% Falkland Merino, 25% Gotland wool, 780 yds / 650 m – 100 g), colourway Light Grey as main colour (MC). Or approx. 660 yds / 600 m of light fingering weight yarn.

1 skein of No. 4 by G-Uld (75% Falkland Merino, 25% Gotland wool, 780 yds / 650 m – 100 g), colourway Madder as contrasting colour (CC). Or approx. 660 yds / 600 m of light fingering weight yarn.

Needles: US 2.5 / 3 mm 32" / 80 cm circular needles or size needed to obtain the gauge.

Notions: Tapestry needle.

GAUGE

26 sts x 52 rows to 4" / 10 cm on US 2.5 / 3 mm needles in garter stitch, after blocking.

SPECIAL TECHNIQUE

Attached I-cord edging

Provisionally CO 4 sts and knit one row of i-cord (i.e. slide the stitches back to left needle and knit them again). *Slide stitches again to left needle and knit until 1 stitch of the i-cord remains. Slip the last stitch purlwise. Work a yarn over and go through the edge of the knitting, pick up and knit a stitch. Pass the 2nd and 3rd stitches (the slipped stitch and the yarn over) over the picked up stitch.* You should now have 4 stitches on the needle. Continue as established until you have worked around the edge and reach the CO stitches of the i-cord. BO the ends of i-cord using Kitchener stitch.

DIRECTIONS

FIRST TRIANGLE, STRIPED PART

Note: Weigh your skeins before starting to make sure you make to most out of your yarn in case your gauge/yardage/yarn differs from the one shown in the sample.

Using circular needles and MC, CO 3 stitches.
SET-UP ROW (MC, RS): K1, k1fb, k1.
SET-UP ROW (MC, WS): Knit to end.

Begin striping
ROW 1 (CC, RS): K1, k1fb, knit to end.
ROW 2 (CC, WS): Knit to end.
ROW 3 (MC, RS): K1, k1fb, knit to end.
ROW 4 (MC, WS): Knit to end.

Repeat rows 1–4, 98 more times (or until you have used almost half of each skein if you are working with different yarn/yardage/gauge). Work rows 1 and 2 once after the repeats.

You should have 203 sts on needles.

SECOND TRIANGLE, COLOUR 2

Cut MC. Continue with CC only.
ROW 5 (RS): K1fbf, turn work.
ROW 6 (WS): K3.
ROW 7: Knit to 2 sts before previous turning point, k1fb, slip the next st knitwise, work a yarn over, k1 (from the live stitches of the first triangle), pass the the slipped stitch and the yo over the knitted stitch. Turn work. Note: Fist time working this row, you only knit 1 stitch before the increase.
ROW 8: Knit to end.
ROW 9: Knit to 2 sts before previous turning point, k1fb, slip the next st knitwise, work a yarn over, k2tog (from the live stitches of the first triangle), pass the the slipped stitch and the yo over the k2tog-stitch. Turn work.
ROW 10: Knit to end.

Repeat rows 7–10 until you have used up all stitches of the first triangle. You should have 138 sts on needles, approx. ¾ of the stitches from the end of first triangle. End with the last RS row.

THIRD TRIANGLE, COLOUR 1

Cut CC. Continue with MC only. You will work the joining on WS from now on from the live stitches on the second triangle.

SET-UP ROW (WS): K1fbf, turn work.
ROW 11 (RS): K3.
ROW 12 (WS): K1, k1fb, knit to last st before previous turning point, slip the next st knitwise, work a yarn over, k1 (from the live stitches of the second triangle), pass the the slipped stitch and the yo over the knitted stitch. Turn work.
ROW 13 (RS): Knit to end.

Repeat rows 12–13 until you have used up all stitches of the second triangle. Note: End with the last WS row, row 12. You should have 138 sts on needles, the same amount as on the first triangle, approx. ¾ of the stitches from the end of first triangle.

FINISHING

Work attached i-cord edging around the entire shawl, see Special Technique section.

Start with the striped cast-on corner and CC, work attached i-cord for the lower edge in approx. a ratio of 2 rows of i-cord for every 3 rows of the shawl edge. When moving onto the edge of the second triangle, work i-cord in approx. a ratio of 1 row for every 2 rows. When moving onto the edge of the third triangle, change i-cord colour to MC and keep that ratio for the top edge too. Change yarn to CC again for the striped part. Join the ends of the i-cord using Kitchener stitch.

Weave in all remaining yarn ends and block the shawl to measurements and shape using wires and pins.

Note: You can also work i-cord using just one colour or using the colour of the triangle, even work it striped if you prefer. If you have a different yarn and gauge, make sure i-cord lays flat. You may need to change the ratio of i-cord accordingly.

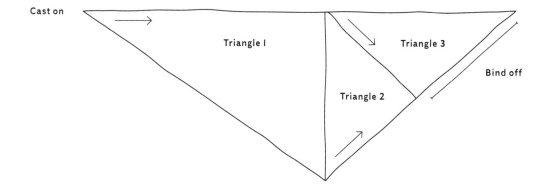

Käpy

Walking in the woods and looking for little treasures. In my little basket you can find some feathers, a few stones, a couple of pine cones and, if I am very lucky, some mushrooms. I have never felt a strong longing for the woods, but I'm so happy with these little adventures.

This cardigan is a mixture of a shawl and a cardigan, with generous positive ease and a very loose fit. The KÄPY cardigan has wide, overlapping fronts, with no closure. A deep, autumnal colour is paired with delicate lace details and crisp stripes.

SIZES

1 (2, 3, 4, 5, 6, 7, 8, 9)

Shown in size 3. Recommended ease: 8–10" / 20–25 cm of positive ease.

To fit a bust circumference of approx.: 30 (34, 38, 42, 46, 50, 54, 58, 62)" / 75 (85, 95, 105, 115, 125, 135, 145, 155) cm.

FINISHED MEASUREMENTS

Back Width at Widest Part (low back and hem): 22 (24, 26, 28, 30, 32, 34, 36, 38)" / 55 (60, 65, 70, 75, 80, 85, 90, 95) cm.

Upper Arm Circumference: 11 (11.5, 12.5, 13.5, 14.5, 16, 17.5, 19, 21)" / 27 (29, 31, 33, 36, 40, 44, 48, 52) cm.

Full Length (neck to hem): 24 (24, 28, 28, 28, 28, 32, 32, 32)" / 60 (60, 70, 70, 70, 70, 80, 80, 80) cm.

Sleeve Length (from underarm) (all sizes): 14" / 35 cm.

Cuff Circumference: 7 (7.5, 8, 9, 10, 11, 12, 13, 14.5)" / 18 (19, 20, 24, 25, 28, 32, 34, 36) cm.

MATERIALS

Yarn: 7 (7, 8, 8, 9, 9, 9, 10, 10) skeins of Soka'pii by The Farmers Daughter Fibers (100% Rambouillet wool, 248 yds / 227 m – 50 g), colourway Eagle Eye as main colour (MC). Or approx. 1560 (1680, 1780, 1880, 1990, 2090, 2200, 2320, 2440) yds / 1430 (1540, 1630, 1720, 1820, 1910, 2010, 2120, 2230) m of fingering weight yarn.

2 (2, 2, 3, 3, 3, 3, 3, 3) skeins of Soka'pii by The Farmers Daughter Fibers (100% Rambouillet wool, 248 yds / 227 m – 50 g), colourway Natural as contrasting colour (CC). Or approx. 380 (420, 460, 500, 540, 580, 620, 660, 700) yds / 350 (380, 420, 460, 500, 530, 570, 600, 640) m of fingering weight yarn.

Needles: US 2 / 2.75 mm 32" / 80 cm circular needles and US 4 / 3.5 mm 32" / 80 cm circular needles and DPNs for sleeves in each size if not using magic loop method for short circumference knitting, or size needed to obtain the gauge.

Notions: Stitch markers, two locking stitch markers or safety pins, tapestry needle, row counter.

GAUGE

24 sts x 26 rows to 4" / 10 cm on mm needles in Stockinette stitch, after blocking.

STITCH PATTERN

Lace
Worked over 16 sts and 32 rows.
Row 1 (RS): P1, k4, k2tog, k1, yo, p1, yo, k1, ssk, k4.
Row 2 and all WS rows: P7, k1, p7, k1.
Row 3: P1, k4, k2tog, yo, k1, p1, k1, yo, ssk, k4.
Row 5: P1, ssk, k3, yo, k2, p1, k2, yo, k3, k2tog.
Row 7: P1, ssk, k2, yo, k3, p1, k3, yo, k2, k2tog.
Row 9: P1, ssk, k5, yo, p1, yo, k5, k2tog.
Row 11: P1, ssk, k4, yo, k1, p1, k1, yo, k4, k2tog.
Row 13: P1, k3, k2tog, yo, k2, p1, k2, yo, ssk, k3.
Row 15: P1, k2, k2tog, yo, k3, p1, k3, yo, ssk, k2.
Row 17: P1, yo, k1, ssk, k4, p1, k4, k2tog, k1, yo.
Row 19: P1, k1, yo, ssk, k4, p1, k4, k2tog, yo, k1.
Row 21: P1, k2, yo, k3, k2tog, p1, ssk, k3, yo, k2.
Row 23: P1, k3, yo, k2, k2tog, p1, ssk, k2, yo, k3.
Row 25: P1, yo, k5, k2tog, p1, ssk, k5, yo.
Row 27: P1, K1, yo, k4, k2tog, p1, ssk, k4, yo, k1.
Row 29: P1, k2, yo, ssk, k3, p1, k3, k2tog, yo, k2.
Row 31: P1, k3, yo, ssk, k2, p1, k2, k2tog, yo, k3.

NOTE

Read the chart from bottom to top and from right to left.

DIRECTIONS

LACE PANEL

Using US 4 / 3.5 mm needles and MC, provisionally CO 85 (85, 101, 101, 101, 101, 117, 117, 117) sts. Work lace as follows.
Row 1 (RS): K2, work row 1 of lace to last 3 sts, p1, k2.
Row 2 (WS): P2, k1, work the next row of lace to last 2 sts, p2.
Row 3 (RS): K2, work the next row of lace to last 3 sts, p1, k2.
Row 4 (WS): P2, k1, work the next row of lace to last 2 sts, p2.

Repeat rows 3–4 until the piece measures 32 (36, 40, 44, 48, 52, 58, 62, 68)" / 80 (88, 98, 108, 120, 130, 144, 156, 170) cm from cast-on edge, ending with a WS row.

Join for lower body
Place safety pins or locking stitch markers to indicate the parts left for sleeves on the long edge of the lace: Place the first pin after 7 (7.5, 8.5, 9.5, 10.5, 12, 13.5, 15, 17)" / 17 (19, 21, 24, 27, 30, 34, 38, 42) cm and the second 7 (7.5, 8.5, 9.5, 10.5, 12, 13.5, 15, 17)" / 17 (19, 21, 24, 27, 30, 34, 38, 42) cm before the end. That will make the picking up the stitches for the lower body easier.

Joining rnd (RS): Knit the lace sts, CO 24 sts (all sizes) using backwards loop CO, pick up and knit 108 (120, 132, 144, 156, 168, 180, 192, 204) sts for back from the long edge between the two safety pins, CO 24 sts (all sizes) using backwards loop CO, knit the provisional CO stitches.
Next row (WS): Knit to end.

LOWER BODY

Continue with stitches on needle and work in garter stitch and stripes: two rows in CC, two rows in MC. Continue until the striped part measures 10 (10, 10, 11, 11, 11, 12, 12, 12)" / 25 (25, 25, 27, 27, 27, 30, 30, 30) cm, ending with a MC stripe. BO sts on next row (RS).

SLEEVES

Using US 4 / 3.5 mm, attach MC to centre of underarm cast-on edge. Pick up and knit 12 sts from underarm cast-on edge (all sizes), pick up and knit 42 (45, 51, 57, 63, 72, 81, 90, 102) sts along sleeve opening to underarm cast-on edge, pick up and knit 12 sts to centre of underarm. You should have 66 (69, 75, 81, 87, 96, 105, 114, 126) sts on needles.

Continue even in St st until the sleeve measures 2" / 5 cm from underarm.

Begin sleeve decreases
Dec rnd: K2tog, knit to last 2 sts, ssk.

Repeat the decrease round on every 10th (10th, 10th, 10th, 8th, 8th, 8th, 8th, 8th) round 8 (8, 9, 9, 9, 10, 10, 10, 10) more times. 48 (51, 55, 61, 67, 74, 83, 92, 104) sts on needles. Work in St st until the sleeve measures 12" / 30 cm.

Change to US 2 / 2.75 mm needles. Work 2" / 5 cm in garter stitch. BO sleeve sts on next round.

FINISHING

Weave in all yarn ends and block the cardigan using your preferred method.

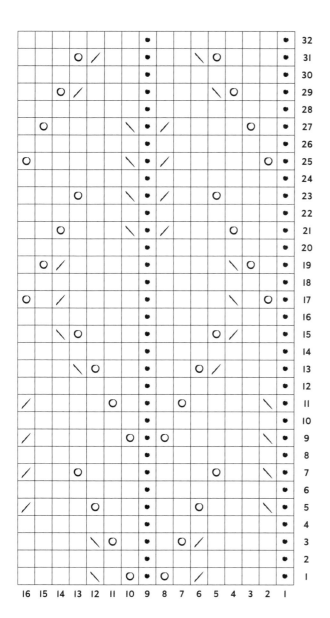

Knit on RS, purl on WS

● Purl on RS, knit on WS

\ Ssk

/ K2tog

O Yo

Ida

Do you see that stream of cold water running down the river? After being held below the frozen surface for months and months, the water is just breaking through the ice, telling it to melt away and letting spring work its magic. This moment is exhilarating! It gives me hope of the warm time ahead.

IDA, a set of a beanie and cowl, resembles that very moment. You can still see snow flowers, but the blue water is already coming through. The beanie is worked from the brim up in one piece. The cowl is worked sideways in the round and then joined with Kitchener stitch, grafting the provisional CO and live stitches together.

SIZES – BEANIE

1 (2, 3)

Shown in size 1.

SIZE – COWL

One Size

FINISHED MEASUREMENTS

Hat
Circumference at brim: 18 (20, 22)" / 45 (50, 55) cm.
Length: 14" / 35 cm.

Cowl
Tube circumference: 17.75" / 44 cm.
Length (then joined for a circle): 51" / 128 cm.

MATERIALS (FOR BOTH HAT AND COWL)

Yarn: 2 (2, 3) skeins of Aphrodite DK by Lain'amourée (70% baby alpaca, 20% silk, 10% cashmere, 240 yds / 225 m – 100 g), colourway Eblouie par la nuit as MC. Or approx. 460 (475, 500) yds / 420 (440, 460) m of DK weight yarn.

2 (2, 3) skeins of Aphrodite DK by Lain'amourée (70% baby alpaca, 20% silk, 10% cashmere, 240 yds / 225 m – 100 g), colourway Les pieds dans la sable as CC. Or approx. 460 (475, 500) yds / 420 (440, 460) m of DK weight yarn.

Needles: US 2.5 / 3 mm and US 3 / 3.5 mm 16" / 40 cm circular needles (for hat). US 7 / 4.5 mm 16" / 40 cm circular needles (for cowl). Choose size needed to obtain the gauge.

Notions: Stitch markers, tapestry needle, waste yarn (for provisional CO) and spare circular needle for grafting.

GAUGE

Beanie
28 sts x 36 rows to 4" / 10 cm on US 2.5 / 3 mm needles in rib stitch, after blocking.

Cowl
20 sts x 24 rows to 4" / 10 cm on US 7 / 4.5 mm needles in Stockinette stitch, after blocking.

SPECIAL ABBREVIATION

SK2PO: Slip 1 stitch as if to knit, knit next 2 stitches together, pass slipped stitch over. (2 sts dec'd)

STITCH PATTERN

Fishtail Lace for the cowl
Multiple of 8 sts, in the round.
Row 1 (RS): *K1, yo, k2, sk2po, k2, yo*, rep *–*.
Row 2 (RS): Knit all stitches.
Row 3: *K2, yo, k1, sk2po, k1, yo, k1*, rep *–*.
Row 4: Knit all stitches.
Row 5: *K3, yo, sk2po, yo, k2*, rep *–*.
Row 6: Knit all stitches.

SPECIAL TECHNIQUE

Kitchener Stitch
Place the provisionally CO edge to spare circ needle and hold the needles with live stitches parallel. Thread a tapestry needle with MC. Insert the tapestry needle through the first stitch on the front needle as if to purl. Pull the yarn through, leaving a tail that you will weave in later. Leave the stitch on the front needle. Insert the tapestry needle through the first stitch on the back needle as if to knit, pull the yarn through and leave the stitch on the back needle.

Insert the tapestry needle through the first stitch on the front needle as if to knit, pull the yarn through and remove the stitch from the front needle. Insert the tapestry needle through the first stitch on the front needle as if to purl and pull the yarn through. Leave the stitch on the front needle. Insert the tapestry needle through the first stitch on the back needle as if to purl, pull the yarn through and remove the stitch on the back needle. Insert the tapestry needle through the first stitch on the back needle as if to knit and pull the yarn through. Leave the stitch on the back needle. Repeat *–* until all stitches on needles have been worked. Note: Keep in mind that you are making an extra row of knitting rather than a seam, don't pull the thread too tightly.

DIRECTIONS

BEANIE

Using US 2.5 / 3 mm circular needles and MC, using a tubular CO cast on 126 (140, 154) stitches. Carefully join in round and work in 1 x 1 ribbing.

When the ribbing measures 7.5" / 19 cm, change to US 3 / 3.5 mm needles.

Attach CC. Begin striping in St st.

Work striping as follows: Work 4 rounds in MC, 4 rounds in CC.

When the beanie measures 11" / 28 cm from the brim, begin crown decreases.
Note: Keep striping as established, 4 rounds in MC and 4 rounds in CC.

Set-up rnd for decreases: SM, ssk, knit 28 (31, 34), k2tog, PM, ssk, knit 27 (31, 33), k2tog, PM, knit 28 (31, 34), k2tog, PM, knit 27 (31, 33), k2tog.

Knit the next round (keep striping continuous).

Decrease rnd: *SM, ssk, knit to 2 sts before next m, k2tog*, repeat *–* 3 more times.

Work the decreases on every second round until 10 (12, 10) sts remain. Cut yarn leaving a good tail and thread through the remaining stitches twice. Fasten securely to WS.

COWL

Using CC and circular needles, provisionally CO 88 sts. Carefully join in round without twisting your stitches and place a marker for BOR. Knit two rounds and then begin lace pattern.

Work a total of 16 repeats of the lace.

Work 4 more rounds in CC.

Then begin striping: Knit 4 rounds in MC, then 4 rounds in in CC.

Continue striping until the cowl measures 51" / 128 cm, ending with 1 round of CC. Then release the provisional CO edge to a spare circ needle, and join the two ends using Kitchener stitch.

Note: Weave in all the yarn ends on WS before grafting the two ends together.

FINISHING

Weave in all yarn ends and block the cowl and beanie using your preferred method.

Minna

This shawl is inspired by the ripples on water. See how the water moves, never stopping, always flowing? This is the element I am so often drawn to. With water there is no end, there is no obstacle too hard.

MINNA is worked in one piece as a bias triangle shawl. The beginning is worked in even stripes, and in the final brioche section you make a series of brioche increases and decreases to create a wavelike movement.

SIZE
One Size

FINISHED MEASUREMENTS

Wingspan: 104" / 264 cm.
Depth (at deepest point): 27.5" / 70 cm.

MATERIALS

Yarn: 2 skeins of Singles by Life in the Long Grass (100% SW Merino, 400 yds / 366 m – 100 g), colourway Night as main colour (MC). Or approx. 760 yds / 695 m of fingering weight yarn.

2 skeins of Singles by Life in the Long Grass (100% SW Merino, 400 yds / 366 m – 100 g), colourway Wheat as contrasting colour (CC). Or approx. 700 yds / 640 m of fingering weight yarn.

Needles: US 4 / 3.5 mm 32" / 80 cm circular needles or size needed to obtain the gauge.

Notions: Stitch markers, tapestry needle.

GAUGE

22 sts x 44 rows to 4" / 10 cm on US 4 / 3.5 mm needles in brioche stitch, after blocking.

SPECIAL ABBREVIATIONS AND TECHNIQUES

BRK: Brioche knit. Knit slipped stitch together with its yarn over.

BRKYOBRK: Brioche knit, yarn over, brioche knit into the same stitch. (2 sts inc'd)

BRLSL: A 2 stitch decrease that slants to the left, involving 3 stitches: Slip the first stitch knitwise together with its yarn over, brk the following two stitches together, pass the slipped stitch over together with its yarn over. (2 sts dec'd)

BRRSL: A 2 stitch decrease that slants to the right, involving 3 stitches: Slip the first stitch knitwise together with its yarn over, knit the next stitch, pass the slipped stitch over together with its yarn over, place stitch on left needle, and pass the following stitch over with its yarn over. Place stitch back on right needle. (2 sts dec'd)

BRP: Brioche purl. Purl slipped stitch together with its yarn over.

I-Cord BO
Continue with the attached i-cord edging. RS: *K3, slip the next stitch kwise, knit the next stitch (first of the live stitches of bottom edge). Pass the 4th stitch over the knitted edge stitch. Slide the just knitted 4 stitches back onto left needle.* Repeat *–* until you have worked all bottom edge stitches and reach the other end of the i-cord (8 sts remain). Graft the two ends of the i-cord together using Kitchener stitch.

SL1YO: With yarn in front slip 1 stitch purlwise, yarn over.

NOTE

In the first part the stripe sequence is worked over 54 rows: 50 rows worked in MC followed by 4 rows in CC.

DIRECTIONS

FIRST PART OF BRIOCHE

Using circular needles and MC, provisionally CO 4 stitches.

Note: You will first work a bit of i-cord to begin your shawl.

Work 5 rows of I-cord: *Knit the sts and slide or slip them back onto the left tip of the needle*, repeat *–* 4 times. Slide/slip the sts back onto the left tip, knit 4 sts, pick up and knit 3 sts from the vertical edge of your I-cord (1 st/row and the extra rows for the I-cord ends), place the provisionally cast-on sts onto the left tip of your circular and knit those 4 sts. You should have 11 sts on needles, 4 on each end for I-cord finishing and 3 picked up from length of the I-cord.

SET-UP ROW (MC, WS): Slip the first 4 sts wyif, sl1yo, k1, sl1yo, slip the last 4 sts wyif.

ROW 1 (MC, RS): K4, slide the sts back onto left-hand needle, k4 (i-cord edge sts for a second time), brkyobrk, *sl1yo, brk*, repeat *–* to last 4 sts, k4. Note: First time working row 1, you only have 2 sts in-between the increase and the edge I-cord. On later repeats the stitch count increases.

ROW 2 (MC, WS): Slip the first 4 sts wyif, sl1yo, *brk, sl1yo*, repeat *–* to last 4 sts, slip the last 4 sts wyif.

ROW 3: K4, slide the sts back onto left-hand needle, k4, brkyobrk, *sl1yo, brk1*, repeat *–* to last 4 sts, k4.

ROW 4: Slip the first 4 sts wyif, sl1yo, *brk1, sl1yo*, repeat *–* to last 4 sts, slip the last 4 sts wyif.

ROW 5: K4, slide the sts back onto left-hand needle, k4, brkyobrk, *sl1yo, brk*, repeat *–* to last 8 sts, sl1yo, brLsl , k4.

ROW 6: Slip the first 4 sts wyif, sl1yo, *brk1, sl1yo*, repeat *–* to last 4 sts, slip the last 4 sts wyif.

Rep rows 1–6, 8 more times. You should have 47 sts on needles.

BRIOCHE STRIPING

Begin striping. Attach CC. Continue repeating rows 1–6, but work the next 4 rows in CC, then the following 50 rows in MC. Continue as established until you have 5 CC stripes in your shawl. After the last CC stripe, work 44 more rows in MC. 223 sts total. Cut MC.

BRIOCHE TEXTURE
Re-attach CC.

ROW 1 (CC, RS): K4, slide the sts back onto left-hand needle, k4, brkyobrk, sl1yo, brk, sl1yo, *brkyobrk, PM, (sl1yo, brk) 7 times, sl1yo, PM, brLsl, (sl1yo, brk) 8 times, sl1yo, brRsl, PM, (sl1yo, brk) 7 times, sl1yo, PM, brkyobrk, (sl1yo, brk) 7 times, sl1yo*, repeat *–* once, brkyobrk, PM, (sl1yo, brk) 7 times, sl1yo, PM, brLsl, (sl1yo, brk) 8 times, sl1yo, brRsl, PM, (sl1yo, brk) 7 times, sl1yo, PM, brkyobrk, (sl1yo, brk) to last 4 sts, k4.

ROW 2 AND ALL FOLLOWING WS ROWS: Slip the first 4 sts wyif, sl1yo, *brk, sl1yo*, repeat *–* to last 4 sts slipping markers, slip the last 4 sts wyif.

ROW 3: K4, slide the sts back onto left-hand needle, k4, brkyobrk, sl1yo, (brk, sl1yo) to 1 st before marker, *brkyobrk, SM, (sl1yo, brk) 7 times, sl1yo, SM, brLsl, (sl1yo, brk) 6 times, sl1yo, brRsl, SM, (sl1yo, brk) 7 times, sl1yo, SM, brkyobrk, (sl1yo, brk) to 2 sts before marker, sl1yo*, repeat *–* once, brkyobrk, SM, (sl1yo, brk) 7 times, sl1yo, SM, brLsl, (sl1yo, brk) 6 times, sl1yo, brRsl, SM, (sl1yo, brk) 7 times, sl1yo, SM, brkyobrk, (sl1yo, brk) to last 4 sts, k4.

ROW 5: K4, slide the sts back onto left-hand needle, k4, brkyobrk, sl1yo, (brk, sl1yo) to 1 st before marker, *brkyobrk, SM, (sl1yo, brk) 7 times, sl1yo, SM, brLsl, (sl1yo, brk) 4 times, sl1yo, brRsl, SM, (sl1yo, brk) 7 times, sl1yo, SM, brkyobrk, (sl1yo, brk) to 2 sts before marker, sl1yo*, repeat *–* once, brkyobrk, SM, (sl1yo, brk) 7 times, sl1yo, SM, brLsl, (sl1yo, brk) 4 times, sl1yo, brRsl, SM, (sl1yo, brk) 7 times, sl1yo, SM, brkyobrk, (sl1yo, brk) to last 8 sts, sl1yo, brLsl, k4.

ROW 7: K4, slide the sts back onto left-hand needle, k4, brkyobrk, sl1yo, (brk, sl1yo) to 1 st before marker, *brkyobrk, SM, (sl1yo, brk) 7 times, sl1yo, SM, brLsl, (sl1yo, brk) 2 times, sl1yo, brRsl, SM, (sl1yo, brk) 7 times, sl1yo, SM, brkyobrk, (sl1yo, brk) to 2 sts before marker, sl1yo*, repeat *–* once, brkyobrk, SM, (sl1yo, brk) 7 times, sl1yo, SM, brLsl, (sl1yo, brk) 2 times, sl1yo, brRsl, SM, (sl1yo, brk) 7 times, sl1yo, SM, brkyobrk, (sl1yo, brk) to last 4 sts, k4.

ROW 9: K4, slide the sts back onto left-hand needle, k4, brkyobrk, sl1yo, (brk, sl1yo) to 1 st before marker, *brkyobrk, SM, (sl1yo, brk) 7 times, sl1yo, SM, brLsl, sl1yo, brRsl, SM, (sl1yo, brk) 7 times, sl1yo, SM, brkyobrk, (sl1yo, brk) to 2 sts before marker, sl1yo*, repeat *–* once, brkyobrk, SM, (sl1yo, brk) 7 times, sl1yo, SM, brLsl, sl1yo, brRsl, SM, (sl1yo, brk) 7 times, sl1yo, SM, brkyobrk, (sl1yo, brk) to last 4 sts, k4.

ROW 11: K4, slide the sts back onto left-hand needle, k4, brkyobrk, sl1yo, (brk, sl1yo) to 1 st before marker, *brkyobrk, SM, (sl1yo, brk) 7 times, sl1yo, SM, brLsl, RM, (sl1yo, brk) to 1 st before marker, sl1yo, SM, (sl1yo, brk) to 2 sts before marker, sl1yo*, repeat *–* once, brkyobrk, SM, (sl1yo, brk) 7 times, sl1yo, SM, brLsl, RM, (sl1yo, brk) 7 times, sl1yo, SM, (sl1yo, brk) to last 8 sts, sl1yo, brLsl, k4.

ROWS 13 AND 15: K4, slide the sts back onto left-hand needle, k4, brkyobrk, sl1yo, (brk, sl1yo) to 1 st before marker, *brkyobrk, SM, (sl1yo, brk) 7 times, sl1yo, SM, brLsl, (sl1yo, brk) to 1 st before marker, sl1yo, SM, (sl1yo, brk) to 2 sts before marker, sl1yo*, repeat *–* once, brkyobrk, SM, (sl1yo, brk) 7 times, sl1yo, SM, brLsl, (sl1yo, brk) to 1 st before marker, sl1yo, SM, (sl1yo, brk) to last 4 sts, k4.

ROW 17: K4, slide the sts back onto left-hand needle, k4, brkyobrk, *sl1yo, brk*, repeat *–* to last 8 sts, sli1yo, brLsl, k4.

ROWS 19 and 21: K4, slide the sts back onto left-hand needle, k4, brkyobrk, *sl1yo, brk*, repeat *–* to last 4 sts, k4.

ROW 23: K4, slide the sts back onto left-hand needle, k4, brkyobrk, sl1yo, (brk, sl1yo) to 3 st before marker, *brRsl, SM, (sl1yo, brk) 7 times, sl1yo, SM, brkyobrk, (sl1yo, brk) to 1 st before marker, sl1yo, SM, (sl1yo, brk) to 4 sts before marker, sl1yo*, repeat *–* once, brRsl, SM, (sl1yo, brk) 7 times, sl1yo, SM, brkyobrk, (sl1yo, brk) to 1 st before marker, sl1yo, SM, (sl1yo, brk) to last 8 sts, sl1yo, brLsl, k4.

ROWS 25 AND 27: K4, slide the sts back onto left-hand needle, k4, brkyobrk, sl1yo, (brk, sl1yo) to 3 st before marker, *brRsl, SM, (sl1yo, brk) 7 times, sl1yo, SM, brkyobrk, (sl1yo, brk) to 1 st before marker, sl1yo, SM, (sl1yo, brk) to 4 sts before marker, sl1yo*, repeat *–* once, brRsl, SM, (sl1yo, brk) 7 times, sl1yo, SM, brkyobrk, (sl1yo, brk) to 1 st before marker, sl1yo, SM, (sl1yo, brk) to last 4 sts, k4.

ROW 29: K4, slide the sts back onto left-hand needle, k4, brkyobrk, sl1yo, (brk, sl1yo) to 3 st before marker, *brRsl, SM, (sl1yo, brk) 7 times, sl1yo, SM, brkyobrk, (sl1yo, brk) to 1 st before marker, sl1yo, SM, (sl1yo, brk) to 4 sts before marker,

sl1yo*, repeat *–* once, brRsl, SM, (sl1yo, brk) 7 times, sl1yo, SM, brkyobrk, (sl1yo, brk) to 1 st before marker, sl1yo, RM, (sl1yo, brk) to last 8 sts, sl1yo, brLsl, k4.

ROW 31: K4, slide the sts back onto left-hand needle, k4, brkyobrk, sl1yo, (brk, sl1yo) to 3 st before marker, *brRsl, SM, (sl1yo, brk) 7 times, sl1yo, SM, brkyobrk, sl1yo, brkyobrk, PM, (sl1yo, brk) to 1 st before marker, sl1yo, SM, brLsl, (sl1yo, brk) to 4 sts before marker, sl1yo*, repeat *–* once, brRsl, SM, (sl1yo, brk) 7 times, sl1yo, SM, brkyobrk, (sl1yo, brk) to last 4 sts, k4.

ROW 33: K4, slide the sts back onto left-hand needle, k4, brkyobrk, sl1yo, (brk, sl1yo) to 3 st before marker, *brRsl, SM, (sl1yo, brk) 7 times, sl1yo, SM, brkyobrk, sl1yo, (brk, sl1yo) to 1 st before marker, brkyobrk, SM, (sl1yo, brk) to 1 st before marker, sl1yo, SM, brLsl, (sl1yo, brk) to 4 sts before marker, sl1yo*, repeat *–* once, brRsl, SM, (sl1yo, brk) 7 times, sl1yo, SM, brkyobrk, (sl1yo, brk) to last 4 sts, k4.

ROW 35: K4, slide the sts back onto left-hand needle, k4, brkyobrk, sl1yo, (brk, sl1yo) to 41 st before marker (note: that should be 1 stitch more than the number of stitches you have between 3rd and 5th marker), brkyobrk, PM, (sl1yo, brk) 7 times, sl1yo, PM, brLsl, (sl1yo, brk) to 4 sts before marker, sl1yo, *brRsl, SM, (sl1yo, brk) 7 times, sl1yo, SM, brkyobrk, sl1yo, (brk, sl1yo) to 1 st before marker, brkyobrk, SM, (sl1yo, brk) to 1 st before marker, sl1yo, SM, brLsl, (sl1yo, brk) to 4 sts before marker, sl1yo*, repeat *–* once, brRsl, SM, (sl1yo, brk) 7 times, sl1yo, SM, brkyobrk, (sl1yo, brk) to last 8 sts, sl1yo, brLsl, k4.

ROWS 37 AND 39: K4, slide the sts back onto left-hand needle, k4, brkyobrk, sl1yo, (brk, sl1yo) to 1 st before marker, brkyobrk, SM, (sl1yo, brk) 7 times, sl1yo, SM, brLsl, (sl1yo, brk) to 4 sts before marker; sl1yo, *brRsl, SM, (sl1yo, brk) 7 times, sl1yo, SM, brkyobrk, sl1yo, (brk, sl1yo) to 1 st before marker, brkyobrk, SM, (sl1yo, brk) to 1 st before marker, sl1yo, SM, brLsl, (sl1yo, brk) to 4 sts before marker, sl1yo*, repeat *–* once, brRsl, SM, (sl1yo, brk) 7 times, sl1yo, SM, brkyobrk, (sl1yo, brk) to last 4 sts, k4.

ROW 41: K4, slide the sts back onto left-hand needle, k4, brkyobrk, sl1yo, (brk, sl1yo) to 1 st before marker, brkyobrk, SM, (sl1yo, brk) 7 times, sl1yo, SM, brLsl, (sl1yo, brk) to 4 sts before marker, sl1yo, *brRsl, SM, (sl1yo, brk) 7 times, sl1yo, SM, brkyobrk, sl1yo, (brk, sl1yo) to 1 st before marker,

154

brkyobrk, SM, (sl1yo, brk) to 1 st before marker, sl1yo, SM, brLsl, (sl1yo, brk) to 4 sts before marker, sl1yo*, repeat *–* once, brRsl, SM, (sl1yo, brk) 7 times, sl1yo, SM, brkyobrk, (sl1yo, brk) to last 8 sts, sl1yo, brLsl, k4.

Rep rows 37–42 once.

ROWS 43 AND 45: K4, slide the sts back onto left-hand needle, k4, brkyobrk, *sl1yo, brk*, repeat *–* to last 4 sts, k4.

ROW 47: K4, slide the sts back onto left-hand needle, k4, brkyobrk, *sli1yo, brk* to last 8 sts, sl1yo, brLsl, k4.

ROWS 49 AND 51: K4, slide the sts back onto left-hand needle, k4, brkyobrk, sl1yo, (brk, sl1yo) to 3 st before marker, brRsl, SM, (sl1yo, brk) 7 times, sl1yo, SM, brkyobrk, (sl1yo, brk) to 2 sts before marker, sl1yo, *brkyobrk, SM, (sl1yo, brk) 7 times, sl1yo, SM, brLsl , sl1yo, (brk, sl1yo) to 3 sts before

ROW 53: K4, slide the sts back onto left-hand needle, k4, brkyobrk, sl1yo, (brk, sl1yo) to 3 st before marker, brRsl, SM, (sl1yo, brk) 7 times, sl1yo, SM, brkyobrk, (sl1yo, brk) to 1 st before marker, sl1yo, *brkyobrk, SM, (sl1yo, brk) 7 times, sl1yo, SM, brLsl , sl1yo, (brk, sl1yo) to 3 sts before marker, brRsl, SM, (sl1yo, brk) to 1 st before marker, sl1yo, SM, brkyobrk, (sl1yo, brk) to 2 sts before marker, sl1yo*, repeat *–* once, brkyobrk, SM, (sl1yo, brk) 7 times, sl1yo, SM, brLsl, (sl1yo, brk) to last 8 sts, sl1yo, brLsl, k4.

ROWS 55 AND 57: K4, slide the sts back onto left-hand needle, k4, brkyobrk, *sl1yo, brk*, repeat *–* to last 4 sts, k4.

On next row (RS) BO all sts using i-cord BO.

FINISHING

Weave in all yarn ends carefully and block the shawl to measurements using your preferred method.

Kaisla

I often think about the salty sea air on a hot summer's day. How the rocks and pebbles feel under bare feet, how the waves hit the shore. How the sun feels on my skin, how the light can be seen even through closed eyes.

KAISLA is worked from the top down in one piece, starting with the front of the upper body, and then continuing with the back of the upper body. To make finishing as minimal-looking as possible, you will work an attached I-cord for the edges after you have finished the dress.

SIZES

1 (2, 3, 4, 5, 6, 7, 8)

Shown in size 3. Recommended ease: 4–6" / 10–15 cm of positive ease.

FINISHED MEASUREMENTS

Bust Circumference: 36 (40, 44, 48, 52, 56, 60, 64)" / 90 (100, 110, 120, 130, 140, 150, 160) cm.
Width of back of the neck: 7.25 (7.25, 7.5, 7.5, 8, 8.5, 8.75, 9.25, 9.5)" / 18 (18, 19, 20, 21, 22, 23, 23.5) cm.
Shoulder width: 2.75 (3, 3, 3.5, 4, 4.5, 5, 5)" / 7 (8, 8, 9, 10, 11, 12, 12) cm.
Depth from shoulder to underarm: 8 (8.5, 9, 9.5, 10, 10.5, 11.5, 12.5)" / 20 (21, 22, 24, 25, 27, 29, 31) cm.
Body Length (from underarm to hem): 25" / 63 cm.

MATERIALS

Yarn: 7 (7, 7, 8, 8, 9, 9, 10, 10) skeins of Sparrow by Quince & Co (100% linen, 168 yds / 155 m – 50 g), colourway Sea Salt as main colour (MC). Or approx. 1060 (1120, 1180, 1260, 1340, 1420, 1500, 1580, 1650) yds / 970 (1020, 1080, 1150, 1230, 1300, 1370, 1450, 1510) m of sport weight yarn.

2 (2, 2, 3, 3, 4, 4, 4) skeins of Sparrow by Quince & Co (100% linen, 168 yds / 155 m – 50 g), colourway Fundi as contrasting colour (CC). Or approx. 240 (280, 330, 380, 440, 490, 550, 600, 660) yds / 220 (260, 300, 350, 400, 450, 500, 550, 600) m of sport weight yarn.

Needles: US 4 / 3.5 mm and US 2 / 3 mm 32" / 80 cm circular needles.

Notions: Stitch markers, stitch holders or waste yarn, tapestry needle.

GAUGE

22 sts x 28 rows to 4" / 10 cm on US 4 / 3.5 mm needles in Stockinette stitch, after blocking.

SPECIAL TECHNIQUE

Attached I-cord edging
Provisionally CO 4 sts and knit one row of i-cord (i.e. slide the stitches back to left needle and knit them again). *Slide stitches again to left needle and knit until 1 stitch of the i-cord remains. Slip the last stitch purlwise. Work a yarn over and go through the edge of the knitting, and pick up a stitch. Pass the 2nd and 3rd stitches (the slipped stitch and the yarn over) over the picked up stitch. You should now have 4 stitches on the needle. Continue as established until you have worked around the edge and reach the CO stitches of the i-cord. BO the ends of i-cord using Kitchener stitch.

NOTE

Work the stripes as follows: 6 rows/rounds of MC followed by 2 rows of CC.

DIRECTIONS

UPPER FRONT

Left shoulder, front
Using MC, cast on 16 (18, 18, 20, 22, 24, 26, 26) sts for shoulder. Work in St st until the piece measures 2" / 5 cm. Begin neck increases on next RS row:

Row 1 (RS): K4, m1l, knit to end.

Repeat row 1 on every RS row for 4 more times.

You should have 21 (23, 23, 25, 27, 29, 31, 31) sts.

Purl one more row.

Cut yarn. Place left shoulder stitches on holder.

Right shoulder, front
Using MC, cast on 16 (18, 18, 20, 22, 24, 26, 26) sts for shoulder. Work in St st until the piece measures 2" / 5 cm. Begin neck increases on next RS row:

Row 2 (RS): Knit to last 4 sts, m1r, knit to end.

Repeat row 2 on every RS row for 4 more times.

You should have 21 (23, 23, 25, 27, 29, 31, 31) sts.

Purl one more row. Keep working yarn attached.

Join shoulders
Knit the right shoulder stitches, cast on 40 (40, 42, 44, 46, 48, 48, 52) sts using a backwards loop CO, knit left shoulder sts. You should have 82 (86, 88, 94, 100, 106, 110, 114) sts for the front. Continue in St st and begin CC striping on next RS row. Work in St st and keep striping (2 rows of CC followed by 6 rows of MC) until the front of the upper body measures 5 (4.75, 4.25, 4.25, 4, 4, 3.75, 3.75)" / 13 (12, 11, 11, 10, 10, 9, 9) cm from shoulder.

Begin underarm increases on next RS row and at the same time keep striping as established.

Row 3 (RS): K4, m1l, knit to last 4 sts, m1r, knit to end.

Repeat row 3, 8 (11, 15, 18, 21, 23, 27, 30) more times on every RS row. End with a WS row.

You should have 100 (110, 120, 132, 144, 154, 166, 176) sts on needles.

Cut both yarns and place sts on holder.

UPPER BACK

Right shoulder, back
Using MC, cast on 16 (18, 18, 20, 22, 24, 26, 26) sts for shoulder. Work 6 rows in St st. Begin neck increases on next RS row:

Row 4 (RS): Knit to last 4 sts, m1r, knit to end.

Repeat row 4 on every RS row for 4 more times. You should have 21 (23, 23, 25, 27, 29, 31, 31) sts. Purl one more row. Cut yarn. Place left shoulder stitches on holder.

Left shoulder, back
Using MC, pick up and knit 16 (18, 18, 20, 22, 24, 26, 26) sts from cast on edge of left shoulder. Work 6 rows in St st. Begin neck increases on next RS row:

Row 5 (RS): K4, m1l, knit to end.

Repeat row 5 on every RS row for 4 more times. You should have 21 (23, 23, 25, 27, 29, 31, 31) sts. Purl one more row. Keep working yarn attached.

Join shoulders
Knit the right shoulder stitches, cast on 40 (40, 42, 44, 46, 48, 48, 52) sts using a backwards loop CO, knit left shoulder sts. You should have 82 (86, 88, 94, 100, 106, 110, 114) sts for the back. Continue in St st and begin CC striping on the same row as you did for the front.

Work in St st and keep striping (2 rows of CC followed by 6 rows of MC) until the upper back measures 5 (4.75, 4.25, 4.25, 4, 4, 3.75, 3.75)" / 13 (12, 11, 11, 10, 10, 9, 9) cm from shoulder.

Begin underarm increases on next RS row and at the same time keep striping as established.
Row 6 (RS): K4, m1l, knit to last 4 sts, m1r, knit to end.

Repeat row 6, 8 (11, 15, 18, 21, 23, 27, 30) more times every RS row. End with a WS row.

You should have 100 (110, 120, 132, 144, 154, 166, 176) sts on needles.

LOWER BODY

Join back and front continuing with the correct colour of striping as follows: Knit back stitches, PM, knit front stitches, PM for BOR.

You should have 200 (220, 240, 264, 288, 308, 332, 352) sts on needles.

Continue in St st and keep striping until the body measures 2" / 5 cm from underarm. Then begin A-line increases.

Increase rnd: SM (BOR), k4, m1l, knit to 4 sts before m, m1r, k4, SM, k4, m1l, knit to 4 sts before m, m1r, k4 to end.

Repeat the increase rnd on every 6th round 21 more times.

88 sts increased, you should have 288 (308, 328, 352, 376, 396, 420, 440) sts on needles.

Continue even in St st and keep striping as established until the piece measures 23" / 58 cm from underarm. Cut CC and continue with MC only.

Shape the hem with short rows as follows:
Short row 1 (RS): SM, knit to 10 sts before next m, w&t.
Short row 2 (WS): Purl to 10 sts before BOR m, w&t.
Short row 3 (RS): Knit to 3 sts before previous wrapped st, w&t.
Short row 4 (WS): Purl to 3 sts before previous wrapped st, w&t.

Repeat short rows 3 and 4, 8 (8, 9, 9, 9, 10, 10, 10) more times.

Knit to marker on next row as follows (RS): *Knit to wrapped st, pick up the wrap (k2tog the wrap with the wrapped st)*, repeat *–* until all wraps before next m are picked up, knit to m. Work short rows for the front:
Short row 5 (RS): SM, knit to 10 sts before next m, w&t.

Short row 6 (WS): Purl to 10 sts before BOR m, w&t.
Short row 7 (RS): Knit to 3 sts before previous wrapped st, w&t.
Short row 8 (WS): Purl to 3 sts before previous wrapped st, w&t.

Repeat short rows 7 and 8, 8 (8, 9, 9, 9, 10, 10, 10) more times.

Knit to end on next row as follows: (RS): *Knit to wrapped st, pick up the wrap (k2tog the wrap with the wrapped st)*, repeat *–* until all wraps before BOR marker are picked up, knit to m.

Change to smaller needles and work in 1 x 1 ribbing. Note: Pick up the last wraps on first round (k2tog or p2tog the wrap with the wrapped stitch). Work 2" / 5 cm in 1 x 1 ribbing and then BO all stitches loosely in ribbing.

FINISHING

Work attached i-cord edging to neckline and around each sleeve opening using MC. See the Special Technique section for more details on attached i-cord. Note: Start sleeve opening i-cords at the underarm and the neck opening from shoulder seam at top of the shoulder (right or left).

Weave in all yarn ends carefully and block the dress to measurements using your preferred method.

Tyven

This shawl is inspired by the phases of the day. Seeing how the sea moves back and forth. Hearing how the sounds change from early morning quietness through the noisy day and finally settle into the stillness of the night.

TYVEN is worked in one piece, starting as a regular triangle. The second part is worked as a reverse diagonal triangle, seamlessly attached to the first part.

SIZE

One Size

FINISHED MEASUREMENTS

Wingspan: 90" / 228 cm.
Depth: 29.5" / 75 cm.

MATERIALS

Yarn: 1 skein of Liina by Aara (50% alpaca, 25% linen, 25% silk, 440 yds / 400 m – 100 g), colourway Väre as main colour (MC). Or approx. 420 yds / 385 m of fingering weight yarn.

1 skein of Liina by Aara (50% alpaca, 25% linen, 25% silk, 440 yds / 400 m – 100 g), colourway Karri as contrasting colour (CC1). Or approx. 420 yds / 385 m of fingering weight yarn.

2 skeins of Hieno by Aara (72% kid mohair, 28% silk, 184 yds /168 m – 20 g), colourway Väre as contrasting colour 2 (CC2). Or approx. 360 yds / 320 m of lace weight yarn.

Needles: US 4 / 3.5 mm 32" / 80 cm circular needles or size needed to obtain gauge.

Notions: Stitch marker, tapestry needle, stitch holder or waste yarn.

GAUGE

18 sts x 36 rows to 4" / 10 cm on US 4 / 3.5 mm needles in garter stitch, after blocking.

DIRECTIONS

PART 1, BASIC TRIANGLE

Using circular needles and MC, provisionally CO 4 stitches.

Note: You will first work a bit of i-cord to begin your shawl.

Work 5 rows of i-cord: *Knit the stitches and slide or slip them back onto the left tip of the needle*, repeat *–* 4 times. Slide/slip the stitches back onto the left tip, knit 4 sts, pick up and knit 3 stitches from the vertical edge of your i-cord (1 stitch/row and the extra rows for the i-cord ends), place the provisionally cast-on stitches onto the left tip of your circular and knit those 4 stitches. You should have 11 stitches on needle, 4 on each end for i-cord finishing and 3 picked up from length of the i-cord.

Set-up row (MC, WS): Slip the first 4 sts wyif, k2, PM, k1, slip the last 4 sts wyif.

Row 1 (MC, RS): K3, k1fb, knit to 1 st before m, k1fb, SM, k1fb, knit to last 5 sts, k1fb, k4.

Row 2 (MC, WS): Slip the first 4 sts wyif, knit to last 4 sts, slip the last 4 sts wyif.

Repeat rows 1 and 2, 58 more times. You should have 247 sts on needles.

Then begin striping: attach CC1 and work Rows 1 and 2 once with CC1, then once with MC. Repeat as established until you have 14 CC1 stripes in your shawl, ending with the last CC1 stripe. You should have 355 sts on needles.

PART 2, WING

Note: You will now work with the first half of stitches only. Place the second half of the stitches onto waste yarn or a stitch holder.

Cut MC and attach CC2, keep CC1 attached.

Set-up Row (CC2 – mohair, RS): K3, k1fb, knit to m, RM, k1 and place the sts remaining on left needle on holder. CO 4 sts using a backwards loop CO, slide the CO stitches back to left needle and *knit the stitches and slide or slip them back onto the left tip of the needle*, repeat *–* twice more. You should have 184 sts on needles, 176 sts on holder.

Set-up row (CC2, WS): Slip the first 4 sts wyif, k2tog, knit to last 4 sts, slip the last 4 sts wyif.

Row 3 (CC2, RS): K3, k1fb, knit to last 6 sts, k2tog, k4, slide the last 4 sts back onto left needle and k4. Note: The extra row of i-cord will help to keep the lower edge from puckering too much.

Row 4 (CC2, WS): Slip the first 4 sts wyif, k2tog, knit to last 4 sts, slip the last 4 sts wyif.

Row 5 (CC1, RS): K3, k1fb, knit to last 6 sts, k2tog, k4.

Row 6 (CC1, WS): Slip the first 4 sts wyif, k2tog, knit to last 4 sts, slip the last 4 sts wyif.

Row 7 (CC2, RS): K3, k1fb, knit to last 6 sts, k2tog, k4.

Row 8 (CC2, WS): Slip the first 4 sts wyif, k2tog, knit to last 4 sts, slip the last 4 sts wyif.

Repeat rows 3–8 until you have 33 sts on needles (or until you run out of CC2). Continue with CC1 only as established until you have 11 sts on needles. BO the 3 sts using an attached i-cord BO for the 3 sts of garter st, then graft the ends of i-cords together using Kitchener st.

I-CORD BO

Move the held stitches back to the circular needles. Using MC, pick up and knit 4 stitches from the backwards loop CO (beginning of the i-cord at the bottom of the first triangle). Work i-cord BO until you have used up all stitches of the garter stitch part. Graft the ends of i-cords together using Kitchener stitch.

FINISHING

Weave in all yarn ends carefully and block the shawl to measurements using your preferred method.

Elin

Whenever I see the sun shining brightly, I reach for my ELIN top.
It has become my go-to sweater in the summer and spring – with
short sleeves and plenty of positive ease, it is so lovely to wear,
yet light enough for the warmer days too.

The Elin sweater is worked easily from the top down in one piece;
it has minimal details, and a lovely relaxed fit.

SIZES

1 (2, 3, 4, 5, 6, 7, 8)

Shown in size 3. Recommended ease: 8–10" / 20–25 cm of positive ease.

FINISHED MEASUREMENTS

Bust Circumference: 38 (42, 46, 50, 54, 58, 62, 66)" / 95 (105, 115, 125, 135, 145, 155, 165) cm.
Upper Arm Circumference: 15 (17, 19, 21, 23.5, 25.5, 27.5, 29.5)" / 37 (42, 47, 52, 58, 64, 69, 74) cm.
Armhole Depth: 11 (12, 13, 14.5, 15.5, 17, 18.5)" / 28 (30, 32, 34, 36, 39, 42, 46) cm.
Body Length (from underarm) (all sizes): 16" / 40 cm.

MATERIALS

Yarn: 1 (1, 1, 2, 2, 2, 2, 2) skein(s) of Nurtured Fine by Julie Asselin (100% fine wool, 780 yds / 708 m – 112 g), colourway Fonte as main colour (MC). Or approx. 690 (730, 780, 850, 915, 975, 1040, 1110) yds / 630 (670, 715, 780, 840, 890, 950, 1015) m of lace weight yarn.

1 (1, 1, 2, 2, 2, 2, 2) skein(s) of Nurtured Fine by Julie Asselin (100% fine wool, 780 yds / 708 m – 112 g), colourway Naturel as contrasting colour (CC). Or approx. 690 (730, 780, 850, 915, 975, 1040, 1110) yds / 630 (670, 715, 780, 840, 890, 950, 1015) m of lace weight yarn.

Needles: US 1.5 / 2.5 mm 32" / 80 cm circular needles and US 2.5 / 3 mm 32" / 80 cm circular needles and DPNs for sleeves in each size if not using magic loop method for short circumference knitting, or size needed to obtain the gauge.

Notions: Stitch markers, stitch holders or waste yarn, tapestry needle.

GAUGE

28 sts and 34 rows to 4" / 10 cm on US 2.5 / 3 mm needles in Stockinette stitch, after blocking.

DIRECTIONS

COLLAR

Using US 1.5 / 2.5 mm circular needles and MC, CO 140 (140, 140, 140, 148, 148, 148, 148) sts using a long-tail CO. Carefully join in round without twisting your stitches and place marker for BOR. Purl 6 rounds.

YOKE

Note about the stripes: Work 36 (38, 40, 40, 42, 42, 44, 44) rounds in each colour for the stripes. Don't calculate the collar rounds to the number, but do add the short row rounds – so calculate the numbers from the back.

Change to US 2.5 / 3 mm circular needles. Note: You will place markers on the first round.

Short Row 1 (RS): SM, m1l, knit 20 (20, 20, 20, 24, 24, 24, 24) sts, m1r, PM, k4, m1l, knit 42 sts (all sizes), m1r, k4, PM, m1l, knit 20 (20, 20, 20, 24, 24, 24, 24) sts, m1r, PM, k4, m1l, k2, w&t.
Short Row 2 (WS): Purl to BOR slipping all other markers, SM, p4, m1rp, p2, w&t.
Short Row 3 (RS): Knit to m, SM, m1l, knit to m, m1r, SM, k4, m1l, knit to 4 sts before next m, m1r, k4, SM, m1l, knit to m, m1r, SM, k4, m1l, knit to wrapped st, PUW, w&t.
Short Row 4 (WS): Purl to beginning of round slipping all other markers, SM, p4, m1rp, purl to wrapped st, PUW, w&t.

Repeat rows 3 and 4, 3 (3, 3, 4, 4, 4, 4, 4) more times. Knit to BOR. Note: On the first time working round 5, remember to pick up the last remaining wraps.

Rnd 5 (RS): *SM, m1l, knit to m, m1r, SM, k4, m1l, knit to 4 sts before next marker, m1r, k4*, repeat *–* once more.
Rnd 6: Knit to end slipping all markers.

Repeat rounds 5 and 6, 36 (43, 50, 57, 63, 71, 77, 84) more times and at the same time remember to change to CC when you have worked 36 (38, 40, 40, 42, 42, 44, 44) rows in MC.

You should have 476 (532, 588, 644, 708, 772, 820, 876) sts on needles.

Divide body and sleeves
Dividing row (RS): SM, place all sts before next marker on holder for sleeve, RM, knit to marker, RM, place all sts before next marker on holder for sleeve, RM, knit to end.

You should have 268 (296, 324, 352, 380, 412, 436, 464) sts on needles for body and 104 (118, 132, 146, 164, 180, 192, 206) sts on each holder for sleeves.

BODY

Continue with the stitches on needle. Work in St st until the body measures 16" / 40 cm and work striping as established. Change to US 1.5 / 2.5 mm needles and work 6 rounds in reverse St st. BO body stitches in reverse St st.

SLEEVES

Place stitches from holder to US 2.5 / 3 mm needles. Keeping the block stripes continuous, attach the right colour to underarm. 104 (118, 132, 146, 164, 180, 192, 206) sts on needles.

Continue even in St st and knit 2" / 5 cm.

Change to US 1.5 / 2.5 mm needles and work 6 rounds in reverse St st. BO sleeve stitches in reverse St st.

FINISHING

Weave in all yarn ends and block the sweater to measurements using your preferred method.

Helene

I can still smell the air flowing, I can still feel how the breeze moves the grass and how the trees whisper. Even if summer is long gone, the memory stays with me forever.

HELENE is all about the lightweight stripes in moody colours. The generous and boxy fit makes this summer top one of my favourite styles to wear.

SIZES

1 (2, 3, 4, 5, 6, 7, 8, 9)

Shown in size 3. Recommended ease: 8" / 20 cm of positive ease.

FINISHED MEASUREMENTS

Bust Circumference: 40 (44, 48, 52, 56, 60, 64, 68, 72)" / 100 (110, 120, 130, 140, 150, 160, 170, 180) cm.
Upper Arm Circumference: 12 (13, 14, 15, 16.5, 18.5, 21, 23, 24.5)" / 30 (33, 35, 38, 41, 46, 52, 57, 61) cm.
Armhole Depth: 9.5 (10.5, 11, 12, 13, 14, 15, 15.5, 16)" / 24 (26, 28, 30, 32, 35, 37, 39, 40) cm.
Body Length (from underarm) (all sizes): 16" / 40 cm.

MATERIALS

Yarn: 2 (2, 2, 2, 2, 3, 3, 3, 3) skeins of Donegal Tweed by Kässäkerho Pom Pom (85% SW Merino, 15% viscose, 440 yds / 400 m – 100 g), colourway Hiili as main colour (MC). Or approx. 560 (635, 720, 820, 920, 1030, 1120, 1200, 1290) yds / 510 (580, 660, 750, 840, 940, 1020, 1100, 1180) m of fingering weight yarn.

2 (2, 2, 2, 2, 3, 3, 3, 3) skeins of Donegal Tweed by Kässäkerho Pom Pom (85% SW Merino, 15% viscose, 440 yds / 400 m – 100 g), colourway Haave as contrasting colour (CC). Or 520 (590, 680, 750, 830, 920, 1010, 1090, 1180) yds / 480 (540, 620, 690, 760, 840, 920, 1000, 1080) m of fingering weight yarn.

Needles: US 1.5 / 2.5 mm 32" / 80 cm circular needles and US 2.5 / 3 mm 32" / 80 cm circular needles and DPNs for sleeves in each size if not using magic loop method for short circumference knitting, or size needed to obtain the gauge.

Notions: Stitch markers, stitch holders or waste yarn, tapestry needle.

GAUGE

26 sts x 36 rows to 4" / 10 cm on US 2.5 / 3 mm needles in Stockinette stitch, after blocking.

STITCH PATTERN

Twisted ribbing
Even number of stitches, worked in the round.
Rnd 1 (RS): *K1 tbl, p1*, rep *–* to end.

DIRECTIONS

COLLAR

Using US 1.5 / 2.5 mm needles and MC, CO 132 sts (all sizes) using a long-tail cast-on. Carefully join in round without twisting your stitches and place marker for beginning of round. Work 12 rounds in 1 x 1 twisted ribbing.

SHOULDER INCREASES

Change to US 2.5 / 3 mm needles and continue with MC.

Set-up Rnd (RS): SM, k30, PM, m1l, k36, m1r, PM, k30, PM, m1l, k36, m1r.
Rnd 1 (RS): *SM, knit to marker, SM, m1l, knit to marker, m1r*, rep *–* once.

Rep rnd 1, 45 (52, 58, 65, 71, 78, 84, 91, 97) more times.

After all shoulder increases you should have 320 (348, 372, 400, 424, 452, 476, 504, 528) sts on needle.

UPPER BACK

Continue with back stitches, stitches between 2nd and 3rd marker, only.

Set-up row (RS): RM, knit and then place the next 30 sts on holder for sleeve, RM, knit to m, RM. Turn work.
Set-up row (WS): P to end of back stitches.

Work 4 rows back and forth in MC.

Decrease row (RS): K4, ssk, knit to last 6 sts, k2tog, k4.

Repeat the decrease row on every 8th row 3 (4, 4, 4, 5, 5, 5, 6, 6) more times and at the same time, 6 more rows after the first decreases, attach CC and begin striping: four rows in CC, two rows in MC.

Continue striping and remaining decreases until the sleeve opening measures 4.5 (5, 5.5, 5.75, 6, 6.5, 7, 7.5, 8, 9)" / 11 (12, 13, 14, 15, 16, 18, 20, 22) cm on the shoulder end. End with a WS row and cut yarns. Place sts on holder or waste yarn.

UPPER FRONT

Continue with front stitches, stitches after 4th marker, only.

Set-up row (RS): Knit and then place the next 30 sts on holder for sleeve, RM, knit front sts (to sts on first holder). Turn work.
Set-up row (WS): P to end of front stitches.

Work 4 rows back and forth in MC.

Decrease row (RS): K4, ssk, knit to last 6 sts, k2tog, k4.

Repeat the decrease row on every 8th row 3 (4, 4, 4, 5, 5, 5, 6, 6) more times and at the same time, 6 more rows after the first decreases, attach CC and begin striping: four rows in CC, two rows in MC.

Continue striping and remaining decreases until the sleeve opening measures 4.5 (5, 5.5, 5.75, 6, 6.5, 7, 7.5, 8, 9)" / 11 (12, 13, 14, 15, 16, 18, 20, 22) cm on the shoulder end. End with a WS row and keep working yarns attached.

Join for lower body
Joining rnd (RS, attach the right colour to keep striping continuous): PM for new beginning of rnd, knit front stitches, CO 8 (10, 10, 10, 12, 12, 12, 14, 14) sts using backwards loop CO, knit back stitches and CO 8 (10, 10, 10, 12, 12, 12, 14, 14) sts using backwards loop CO.

You should have 260 (288, 312, 340, 364, 392, 416, 444, 468) sts on needles for body.

LOWER BODY

Continue even in St st and keep striping as established until the body measures 13.5" / 34 cm from underarm, ending with MC stripe. Cut CC and continue with MC only.

Change to US 1.5 / 2.5 mm needles. Work 2" / 5 cm of 1 x 1 twisted ribbing. BO body sts on next RS round in twisted ribbing.

SLEEVES

Using US 2.5 / 3 mm needles, attach MC to centre of underarm cast-on edge. Pick up and knit 4 (5, 5, 5, 6, 6, 6, 7, 7) sts from underarm CO edge, pick up and knit 28 (31, 33, 36, 39, 42, 47, 52, 58) sts up to stitches on holder, PM, knit 30 sts from holder and pick up and knit 28 (31, 33, 36, 39, 42, 47, 52, 58) sts down to underarm cast on edge, pick up and knit 4 (5, 5, 5, 6, 6, 6, 7, 7) sts to centre of underarm. Join in round and PM for beginning of round.

94 (102, 106, 112, 120, 126, 136, 148, 160) sts on needles.

Shape the sleeves with short rows.
Row 1 (RS): Knit to m, SM, knit to m, SM, k2, w&t.
Row 2 (WS): Purl to m, SM, purl to m, SM, p2, w&t.
Row 3: Knit to m, SM, knit to m, SM, knit to previous wrapped st, PUW, w&t.
Row 4: Purl to m, SM, purl to m, SM, purl to previous wrapped st, PUW, w&t.

Rep rows 3 and 4, 10 (11, 12, 12, 13, 13, 14, 14, 15) more times. Knit to end of round on next row (RS): Knit to m, SM, knit to m, SM, knit to previous wrapped st, PUW, knit to end. Pick up the last remaining wrap on next round.

Work 4 (4, 4, 5, 5, 5, 6, 6, 6) more rounds even. Change to US 1.5 / 2.5 mm needles. Work 2" / 5 cm in 1 x 1 twisted ribbing. BO sleeve sts on next round in twisted ribbing.

FINISHING

Weave in all yarn ends and block the sweater to measurements using your preferred method.

Adventure awaits! I am ready to start another day and another journey! Come with me and together we will find all those paths, all those back alleys, all those stories. This adventure is ours. Let's go!

AINO looks like another striped cardigan, something I am so often drawn to, but it comes with many surprising little details. It has a lovely, relaxed fit, long sleeves and, of course, hidden pockets at the sides. Aino is simply made for all adventures, no matter how big or small they may be.

SIZES

1 (2, 3, 4, 5, 6, 7, 8, 9)

Shown in size 3. Recommended ease: 2–4" / 5–10 cm of positive ease.

FINISHED MEASUREMENTS

Bust Circumference: 34 (38, 42, 46, 50, 54, 58, 62, 66)" / 85 (95, 105, 115, 125, 135, 145, 155, 165) cm.
Upper Arm Circumference: 11 (12, 13, 14, 15.5, 17, 18.5, 20, 22)" / 28 (30, 33, 36, 39, 42, 46, 50, 55) cm.
Armhole Depth: 7.5 (8, 8.5, 9, 10, 11, 11.5, 12, 13)" / 18 (20, 22, 23, 25, 27, 29, 30, 32) cm.
Body Length (from underarm) (all sizes): 17" / 43 cm.
Sleeve Length (from underarm) (all sizes): 18" / 45 cm.
Cuff Circumference: 7 (7.5, 8, 9, 10, 11, 12, 13, 14.5)" / 18 (19, 20, 24, 25, 28, 32, 34, 36) cm.

MATERIALS

Yarn: 2 (3, 3, 3, 4, 4, 4, 5, 5) skeins of Gilliatt by De Rerum Natura (100% Merino, 275 yds / 250 m – 100 g), colourway Fusain as main colour (MC). Or approx. 550 (630, 720, 820, 920, 1020, 1110, 1200, 1270) yds / 500 (580, 660, 750, 840, 930, 1010, 1090, 1160) m of DK weight yarn.

2 (3, 3, 3, 4, 4, 4, 4, 5) skeins of Gilliatt by De Rerum Natura (100% Merino, 275 yds / 250 m – 100 g), colourway Poivre Blanc as contrasting colour (CC). Or approx. 525 (590, 680, 760, 830, 920, 1010, 1090, 1180) yds / 480 (540, 620, 690, 760, 840, 920, 1000, 1080) m of DK weight yarn.

Needles: US 4 / 3.5 mm 32" / 80 cm circular needles and US 7 / 4.5 mm 32" / 80 cm circular needles and DPNs for sleeves in each size if not using magic loop method for short circumference knitting, or size needed to obtain the gauge.

Notions: 6 buttons, 1.5" / 30 mm. Stitch markers, stitch holders or waste yarn, tapestry needle.

GAUGE

18 sts x 26 rows to 4" / 10 cm on US 7 / 4.5 mm needles in Stockinette stitch, after blocking.

DIRECTIONS

COLLAR

Using US 4 / 3.5 mm needles and MC, CO 85 (85, 85, 85, 89, 89, 89, 89) sts with a tubular CO. Do not join.

Work 10 rows in 1 x 1 ribbing.

YOKE

Change to US 7 / 4.5 mm needles and continue with MC. Shape the back of the neck using short rows.

Row 1 (RS): K13 (13, 13, 13, 13, 16, 16, 16, 16), m1r, k1, PM, m1l, k10 (10, 10, 10, 10, 6, 6, 6, 6), m1r, PM, k1, m1l, k37 (37, 37, 37, 37, 43, 43, 43, 43) m1r, k1, PM, m1l, k10 (10, 10, 10, 10, 6, 6, 6, 6), m1r, PM, k1, m1l, k2, w&t.
Row 2 (WS): Purl to last marker, SM, p4, w&t.
Row 3 (RS): *Knit to 1 st before marker, m1r, k1, SM, m1l, knit to marker, m1r, SM, k1, m1l*, repeat *–* once, knit to previous wrapped st, PUW, w&t.
Row 4 (WS): Purl to last marker, SM, purl to previous wrapped st, PUW, w&t.

Repeat last 2 rows 3 (3, 3, 3, 3, 4, 4, 4, 4) more times.

Next row (RS): *Knit to 1 st before marker, m1r, k1, SM, m1l, knit to marker, m1r, SM, k1, m1l*, repeat *–* once, knit to previous wrapped st, PUW, knit to end.
Next row (WS): Purl to last marker, SM, purl to previous wrapped st, PUW, purl to end.

Attach CC and begin striping (four rows in CC, four rows in MC) and continue raglan increases.

Row 1 (RS): *Knit to 1 st before marker, m1r, k1, SM, m1l, knit to marker, m1r, SM, k1, m1l*, repeat *–* once, knit to end.
Row 2 (WS): Purl to end.

Repeat the last 2 rows 13 (15, 17, 20, 23, 27, 31, 34, 39) more times.

Sizes – (2, 3, 4, 5, 6, 7, 8, 9) only
Increase for body.
Row 1 (RS): *Knit to 1 st before marker, m1r, k1, SM, knit to marker, SM, k1, m1l*, rep *–* once, knit to end.

Row 2 (WS): Purl to end.
Repeat the last 2 rows, (3, 4, 6, 7, 4, 4, 6, 5) more time(s).

After all raglan increases you should have 245 (273, 297, 329, 357, 389, 421, 453, 489) sts on needles.

Divide body and sleeves
Dividing row (RS, keep striping continuous): *Knit to marker, SM, place all sts before next marker on holder, RM*, repeat *–* once, knit to end.

You should have 145 (165, 181, 201, 217, 237, 253, 273, 289) sts on needles for body and 50 (54, 58, 64, 70, 76, 84, 90, 100) sts on each holder for sleeves.

BODY

Continue even in St st and keep striping as established until the body measures 7" / 18 cm from underarm.

Pocket openings
Work with left front stitches, stitches before first marker, only. Work 6" / 15 cm in St st and stripes, ending with a WS row. Cut CC and MC.

Work with back stitches, stitches between the markers, only. Work 6" / 15 cm in St st and stripes, keeping the striping continuous and ending with a WS row. Cut CC and MC.

Work with right front stitches, stitches after the last marker, only. Work 6" / 15 cm in St st and stripes, keeping the striping continuous and ending with a WS row. Cut CC and MC.

Keeping striping continuous, re-attach yarn to left front. Continue in St st and striping until the body measures 14" / 35 cm. End with CC stripe. Change to US 4 / 3.5 mm needles.

Divide the stitches in half.
First half: Cut MC and work ribbing in CC.
Second half: Cut CC and work cuff in MC. Work 3" / 8 cm in 1 x 1 ribbing. BO sts on next round using Tubular Bind-Off.

SLEEVES

Place stitches from holder to US 7 / 4.5 mm needles. Keeping the striping continuous, attach the right colour to underarm.

50 (54, 58, 64, 70, 76, 84, 90, 100) sts on needles.
Continue even in St st and keep striping as established until the sleeve measures 3" / 8 cm from underarm. Begin sleeve decreases.

Dec rnd: K2, ssk, knit to last 4 sts, k2tog, k2.

Repeat the decrease round on every 10th (8th, 8th, 6th, 6th, 6th, 6th, 6th, 6th) round 5 (6, 6, 7, 7, 8, 8, 9, 9) more times, keeping striping continuous. 38 (40, 44, 48, 54, 58, 66, 70, 80) sts on needles.

Continue striping until the sleeve measures 14" / 36 cm. End with CC stripe. Change to US 4 / 3.5 mm needles.

Left cuff: Cut MC and work cuff in CC.
Right cuff: Cut CC and work cuff in MC. Work 4" / 10 cm in 1 x 1 ribbing. BO sleeve sts on next round using Tubular Bind-Off.

BUTTONBAND

Right front
Using US 4 / 3.5 mm needles and MC, pick up and knit 105 (109, 113, 117, 121, 125, 129, 133, 137) sts from the front edge. Pick up stitches in ratio of 3 sts every 4 rows. Work 1" / 2.5 cm in 1 x 1 ribbing.

Buttonhole row (RS): (K1, p1) 6 (5, 6, 4, 5, 6, 5, 6, 6) times, k1, *yo, k2tog, (p1, k1) 7 (8, 8, 9, 9, 9, 10, 10, 10) times*, repeat *–* 4 more times, yo, k2tog, (p1, k1) to end.

Work 1" / 2.5 cm in 1 x 1 ribbing. BO sts on next round using Tubular Bind-Off.

Left front
Using US 4 / 3.5 mm needles and CC, pick up and knit 105 (109, 113, 117, 121, 125, 129, 133, 137) sts from the front edge. Pick up stitches in ratio of 3 sts every 4 rows. Work 2" / 5 cm in 1 x 1 ribbing. BO sts on next round using Tubular Bind-Off.

POCKETS

Work left pocket with CC, right pocket with MC.
Using US 7 / 4.5 mm needles and with RS facing, starting from the bottom corner of pocket opening, pick up and knit 22 sts from front edge, pick up and knit 22 sts from back edge. Join

in round. 44 sts on needles.
Work in St st and in the round until the tube measures 4" / 10 cm. Divide stitches evenly on 2 needles and BO sts using 3-needle BO. Turn the pocket to inside the cardigan.

FINISHING

Weave in all yarn ends and block the cardigan to measurements using your preferred method. Seam the bottom ribbing in back. Sew on buttons. Fasten the pockets to WS if needed.

THANK YOU

This book wasn't born in a vacuum, nor was it born out of the thoughts of one single person. It is a collection of many hours, weeks and months of work. It has been shaped by every moment. In the end, the book feels like taking a single word and enriching it into a whole world that is woven around it.

Thank you, Jonna and Sini. You embraced my idea with an open heart, and you have supported me through every stage of the book. Because of you, the book is now so much more than just my original dreams. I am forever grateful to everyone on the team for adding their ideas onto these pages. It is now a whole new world.

Thank you to each yarn company and dyer who supported my book. Your faith in this project is irreplaceable. I hope, from the bottom of my heart, that you like the designs as much as I do. *Stripes* would not have happened without you.

Thank you, Jaana and Maria, for all your help. The sample knits you made are so precious to me. I am grateful for the friendships you have given me as well as all the talent you delivered for these pages.

Thank you to all the test knitters who have worked so many hours on these patterns. Thank you for being so very patient waiting for the book to be finished. Without you, the patterns wouldn't have been half as good as they are now. You have made a huge difference.

Thank you, mom and my grandmothers. My view on both life and craft wouldn't be the same without you. You have shown me that anything is possible, with a little patience and resilience.

Thank you, Iisakki, Aarni and Okko. This book has been in my thoughts for a very long time, through everyday chores as well as accompanying us on our adventures together. Thank you for giving me time to focus on the making of this book. Thank you for patiently watching endless hours of football and different series with me, while I tried to finish all the samples. Now the book is ready.

This edition published in 2023 by Hardie Grant Books,
an imprint of Hardie Grant Publishing
First published in 2021 by Laine Publishing Oy
Published in agreement with Ferly Agency

Hardie Grant Books (Melbourne)
Wurundjeri Country
Building 1, 658 Church Street
Richmond, Victoria 3121

Hardie Grant Books (London)
5th & 6th Floors
52–54 Southwark Street
London SE1 1UN

hardiegrantbooks.com

A catalogue record for this
book is available from the
National Library of Australia

NATIONAL
LIBRARY
OF AUSTRALIA

Stripes
ISBN 978 1 74379 901 7

10 9 8 7 6 5 4 3 2 1

Photographs: Jonna Hietala & Sini Kramer
Layout: Irina Kauppinen
Stylist: Emilia Laitanen
Muah: Miika Kemppainen
Model: Landys / As You Are Agency

Aino: Jeans Chimala.
Kaisla: Jeans Chimala.
Käpy: Jeans A.P.C. Top Tiger of Sweden.
Kyllikki: Jeans A.P.C. Top Tiger of Sweden.
Alli: Dress See by Chloe.
Elin: Trousers writer's own. Sandals Terhi Pölkki.
Ellen: Jacket Prada. Trousers and shirt writer's own.
Kaarna: Trousers writer's own. Jacket Margaret Howell.
    Sandals Terhi Pölkki.
Tyven: Dress Andiata. Clogs Terhi Pölkki.
Varpu: Dress See by Chloé.
Maria: Skirt Sportmax. Shoes Margaret Howell.
    Socks Muji.
Alli green: Trousers A.P.C. T-shirt Acne Studios.
    Jacket Lanvin. Shoes Margaret Howell.
Anni: Skirt Acne Studios.
Helle: Hat Arket. Jeans A.P.C.
Ida: Jacket Prada. Jeans Chimala. Top Tiger of Sweden.
    Shoes Margaret Howell.
Maija: Jeans Chimala.
Maire: Sandals Terhi Pölkki. Socks Muji.
Minna: Jacket Prada. Jeans Chimala. Top Tiger of Sweden.
    Shoes Margaret Howell.
Venny: Trousers Miu Miu. Shirt Acne Studios.
Furniture props: Ornäs.

Colour reproduction by Splitting Image Colour Studio
Printed in China by Leo Paper Products LTD.

The paper this book is printed
on is from FSC®-certified forests
and other sources. FSC® promotes
environmentally responsible, socially
beneficial and economically viable
management of the world's forests.